Michael Smith
Entertains

Michael Smith Entertains

To a great extent party catering has become simpler over the last twenty years. Informal entertaining is now more the order of the day, not least because it releases us from the strictures of the formal dinner party. Yet get-togethers have become more numerous as they have become less formal. Leisure time is fast increasing, so people are looking for more ways to fill these happy hours.

Dietary habits, too, have changed in the 1980s, and for reasons of health, if not of cost, simpler menus are now in vogue. The dinner party is less ostentatious than in the '50s and '60s, when one-upmanship was rife and the fraught hostess produced course after course, wondering why she had ever invited people to her house, since there seemed to be no time to relax to enjoy their company.

With a more liberated outlook on life, an informal buffet party allows host and hostess to bring newcomers into their circle cushioned by a goodly sprinkling of friends known to both sides, if not to each other. It is, in this situation, no longer important to balance even numbers of male and female, and guests are able to move round the edges of a party, so to speak, assessing, in the most relaxed way, whom it would be interesting to talk to. It is possible to move in and out of conversations at will and to eat and drink as much or as little as you like without disappointing your hosts.

But, none of this happens without thought and planning. As with the cook who maintains that she 'guesses' when cooking (but doesn't admit to a visual ability which guesses within a gram of the correct weight!), the host or hostess who claims to have a more than casual approach to entertaining has usually a pretty well-based, if unspoken, idea as to what he or she wants to achieve and just how he or she is going to make it happen. Professional party-givers always work to a plan which perfectly fits their house and their personality.

To help you achieve your own individual best, here are my thoughts on the things you need to consider as you embark on a lifestyle which is to include entertaining in the home at whatever level you decide, at whatever time of day, and wherever the venue.

Michael Smith

Contents

First published in 1986 by Octopus Books Limited, Grosvenor Street, London, England

This edition © 1986 Hennerwood Publications Limited
Text © 1986 Michael Smith
Illustrations © 1986 Octopus Books Limited

ISBN 0 86273 276 X

Printed in England

Introduction

DINNER PARTIES

The best advice I can give to anyone planning to entertain is to design your menu to match your room. I don't mean in colour terms, so much as in space availability. If your dining room table is of a size to seat 6, 7 or 8 comfortably with the appropriate number of matching or alternating chairs, then that is the number you should ask. If you try to squeeze in an extra guest on that small bedroom chair, it throws the table arrangement completely off balance. This can also happen if one of your guests phones up at the last minute to cancel, for whatever reason. Again my advice is to leave well alone. Accept that there will be one less guest and remove the place setting. Unless, of course, you have that all-important friend, the unattached person, who is happy to stand in at very short notice.

FORK LUNCHEONS

This is a relatively new form of home entertaining. At one time, when entertaining informally it was considered fashionable to have a buffet. This meant – and still means for that matter – a variety of cold and hot dishes arranged on a buffet table from which people could make a choice. These dishes included what the French call 'Gros Pièces', large, elaborately garnished joints of meat, whole turkeys, boned game birds, handsome long salmons coated in aspic, as well as an abundance of accompanying salads.

All this was very well when there were enough chairs and tables for everyone to cope with their food easily.

With the disappearance of domestic help and the reduction in the size of the normal home, the scale of this entertaining has gradually become unpracticable.

For a fork luncheon to be successful there are some golden rules, not least of which is the obvious one. The meal must be just what it says it is going to be – a fork lunch – and your invitation should also indicate this fact.

This means that the main dishes should be suitable for eating with a fork and all else offered must be in a similar state of readiness. Breads must be crusted, buttered and cut into fingers or squares, rounds or triangles.

Sauces which are not an integral part of the dish must be few in number; two being the maximum offered, one of these being a chutney, jelly or other relish.

Lettuce, frisée, radicchio and suchlike have to be torn into manageable scraps and ready-tossed in a dressing. Other 'awkward' foods like spaghetti (essentially not a food for an elegant occasion) is at its most manageable when broken into 5–8 cm (2–3 inch) lengths.

Choose 'composite entities' for the starters – by this I mean those dishes which do not need extra items, such as sauces or side-salads, croûtons or other extra elaborate garnishes. An avocado vinaigrette is impossible, for example, whilst you could get away with removing the avocado flesh, mixing it with a thicker dressing and back into the shell ready to be spiked with a fork or scooped up with a spoon.

Any savoury pastry tartlet which you may choose to serve as a starter – and they do make excellent starters, particularly hot ones – should have a mouth-watering crumbling crust; puff pastry invariably needs a knife to cope with the bottom layer.

Chilled soups, of course, are ideal. Think about the notion of serving these in tea cups using a dessertspoon rather than the more cumbersome soup spoon to eat with. A hot clear soup can be sipped straight from the cup as long as you have kept garnishes to a manageable minimum.

Add a base plate, large enough to hold the fork, to the smaller starter plate, separating the two with a tiny paper doily to prevent the dishes sliding and to catch any drips.

Pass any first course to each guest together with a three-ply paper napkin held *under* the base plate. This way it is an easy move to dab wayward drops from lip or lapel without the juggling movements which would be necessary if the napkin were placed between the cup or plate and the base-plate. Think about it!

Linen napkins are best kept for the main course and if the same principle is followed of having the napkin, still folded, *under* the plate this will also prevent any over-hot plate possibly burning the recipient's fingers.

I know that intricately folded and pleated napkins *look* pretty but they do add to the havoc I am trying to help to avoid. Make things as easy for your guests as you can.

Extra 3-ply paper napkins should be strategically placed around the room. This notion, at little extra cost to you, makes life so much easier and more elegant.

DRINKS PARTIES

I first visited the United States in 1976 when I was involved in advising the International Wine and Food Society in their plans for their Bi-centennial celebrations.

It was to be five more years before I crossed that massive country with its ever-changing scenery and people, to experience the California casual way of living.

Up to my crossing the great 'pond', casual – or relaxed – entertaining in England had been 'the Sherry Party' on a Sunday morning where a cheese-straw was about as much sustenance as you would get, or a Cocktail Party, which might consist of an inspired savoury, supplemented by a ubiquitous medley of crisps and nuts.

Yet, and I don't believe in any form of the occult or seeing into the future, I had been serving cocktail, or finger

food, in my own Yorkshire catering business, not that far removed from the American style, as far back as the 1950s.

The drinks party – which is what this type of informal entertaining is now called – is *the* ideal occasion to bring a total mixture of your friends together in large numbers; old and young; family and casual acquaintances, people with differing political and religious views, even friend and foe! – for there is ample opportunity to move around – dip in and out of conversation and, if the party is big enough (and you should always ask more people than your room will hold for a successful affair), it is actually possible for guests to avoid each other if necessary.

The quantity and type of food you need to provide will depend on the time of day you hold your party.

Evening drinks, where people are invited for 6–8 p.m., is a clear indication that you will be going on elsewhere, or back home, for dinner, and cocktail food can be smaller in size – in fact, the canapé is ideal.

A morning party: 11–1 p.m., or a late evening party: 9–midnight, calls for extended food, though not a full buffet, the type of delicacies suggested in the section on American cocktail food, in fact (pages 90 to 97).

WINE

It is better – from a style point of view as well as from a vinicultural and practical aspect – to choose large 200–300 ml (8–10 fl oz) glasses. Fill them to just over the halfway mark. This both gives a feeling of generosity and helps to eliminate spillage, when elbows clash in the happy melée.

A *change* of glass is to be avoided at all costs, except when a toast is to be drunk in, say, Champagne. In which case glasses can be arranged at-the-ready beforehand, in a second area away from the dining throng.

Most guests are happy to help themselves to wine, particularly when they may wish to go cautiously or abstain altogether because they are drivers. It is not for you to say 'No' to guests: it is, however, up to you not to push guests to drink more than they ought to!

When arranging a room for a fork lunch or dinner, don't forget that your guests themselves do take up a deal of space and that one's most elegant and much-loved guest does not necessarily do as he or she is expected to, as they become locked in intimate conversation right by the spot you have chosen to serve your main course, thus blocking any planned traffic flow! Follow the plan on page 9.

A WEDDING IN THE HOME

Most houses can cope with 20–30 people without much moving around of furniture. The wedding reception menu given on page 136 is no more bother than the average Christmas or birthday party you might throw each year. With the guidelines given here, it should all run smoothly on the day, allowing you time to enjoy the occasion, too.

First of all you should organize some help for the whole of the previous day, as well as the day itself, to assist with such jobs as preparing vegetables and washing up. And now is the time to rely on take-away food.

You will need to borrow or hire extra cutlery to make up your own service to the necessary numbers. This should be sorted out at least a week or two beforehand and ideally collected or delivered to your home three days before the wedding, along with the Champagne and/or wine glasses that you will need. It is also a good idea to borrow a dozen tea towels. These can usually be hired from catering service firms and from some laundries. If you draw a blank, then I advise you to buy in at least 6 rolls of paper towels and don't forget such things as extra bin bags, bin liners (see 'washing up' page 15).

The checklist below covers the items you will need for the menu I give on page 136, bearing in mind that it is a fork luncheon and that guests will perch themselves when and where they can, and that all furniture will have been moved; the bulkier pieces upstairs and the smaller pieces put against the wall.

Flowers are essential – but try to keep to my 'all-eggs-in-one-basket' philosophy (page 10). Have one beautiful arrangement in the hall saying 'Welcome, this is a wedding day'. A mixture of pale colours can look stunning: whites, creams, greens, pinks and lemons. I am a great believer in contrasting, even clashing colours, it creates impact and gives depth to the flower arrangements. Each flower needs a background to show itself off to good effect.

THE TABLE ITSELF

Remember that the idea of a buffet table is that people should be able to walk around it, otherwise guests cannot escape once they have filled their plates. So, place the table in a bay window or in the centre of the room. Cover it with your prettiest cloth laid over a toning bed sheet, or make a floorlength cloth of display felt overlaid with copious layers of non-inflammable net. This gives an ethereal and romantic effect, is cheap to do and easy to create. Because you are having a small wedding is no reason to cut down on the glamour of the affair, least of all at the reception.

DRINKS
Decide where you are going to put the table from which you will serve the Champagne. This should be as near as possible to the door where people will be coming in to the reception to greet the bride.

Where a reception is held at home it is better to cut the receiving line right down to either the bridal pair or the brides' parents – for they are the hosts – leaving the couple free to mingle.

Underneath the drinks table lay a piece of industrial plastic or a large bin bag to protect the carpet and have a plastic dustbin ready to hold crushed ice and the bottles.

This, too, should be disguised with a piece of felt or wrapped in a pretty tablecloth and discreetly placed. Secrete a cardboard box under the table to receive any empties, bottle tops, wires, corks and such like.

Have a glass bowl at the side of the glasses to hold the strawberry garnish and have a small glass to hold the cocktail sticks (for spearing the strawberries if guests wish to eat their garnish). Have a small round tray for passing round two or three glasses together; it is dangerous to put too many glasses on a large tray. A couple of linen napkins should be to hand for whoever is pouring the Champagne, to catch drips and mop spills.

ADVANCE PREPARATION
In the preparation stakes, aim to get as much ready two if not three days in advance. Most things, except in the hottest of weathers, will be perfectly alright, and survive well under normal cool conditions if not under refrigeration for two days. The use of a neighbour's refrigerator space would be of great benefit.

Follow the countdown below and everything should be completed ready in time for the great day.

CHECK LIST

- 1 plastic dustbin plus cloth to cover
- empty cardboard boxes, for empty bottles
- 1 smaller box for corks and wires
- 12 tea towels or 6 rolls of paper towels
- 48 Champagne glasses (flutes)
- 6 tumblers for non-drinkers
- 1 large jug for juice or squash
- 1 glass bowl for strawberries
- 1 carton cocktail sticks or tooth picks
- 2 clean napkins or tea towels
- 4 dozen paper cocktail drip mats to slip over the base of glasses to protect surfaces from splashes
- 1 pair pliers to hand for coping with broken wires or Champagne corks
- 1 pourer to fit into Cassis bottle (borrow this from your local pub to make pouring easier)
- 2 packs × 25 cocktail napkins, placed around the rooms
- 2 packs × 12 three or four-ply large paper napkins to slot between the main-course plates
- 2 × 20 cm (8 inch) paper doilys
- 40 large forks
- 40 dessertspoons
- 40 dessert forks
- 40 coffee spoons
- 12 serving spoons
- 12 serving forks
- carving knife and fork for ducks
- carving knife and fork for koulibiacs
- 2 sets salt and pepper
- 48 large plates
- 48 small 18 cm (7 inch) plates
- 48 coffee cups and saucers
- 2 × 600 ml (1 pint) cream jugs
- 2 sugar basins
- 2–3 coffee pots
- 4 large trays for coffee cups
- 2 trays for the canapés
- 2 dishes or platters for the 2 koulibiacs
- 2 meat dishes for the ducks or turkeys
- 2 shallow dishes for beans
- 2 shallow dishes for tomatoes
- 2 large 3.5 litre (6 pint) bowls for potato salad
- 2 large 2 litre (4 pint) glass or china bowls for trifle
- 2 large trays to hold the chocolate creams and 40 individual waxed trifle containers or 2 large 2 litre (3–4 pint) bowls
- 2 baskets to hold split and buttered finger rolls or brioches

RECEPTION COUNTDOWN

1 WEEK BEFORE

- *All* orders for food and drink, flowers and extras to be placed with your shops.
- Have borrowed receptacles to hand.
- Purchase a Duplicate Book: write out your order for each shop, giving them a copy, retaining the second for your own reference. It is also a good idea to write down what you are expecting family and friends to do.
- Arrange the table a week before if you like. Certainly 2 days before.
- Put out, in their place, *all* dishes, piles of plates, napkins etc. Leave room for any flower arrangements, which should be in situ the afternoon before, giving blooms time to settle themselves in, as it were, and open their petals.
- Cover the whole table carefully with a clean sheet.

TWO DAYS BEFORE

- Cook the potatoes. Cool, peel, dice and store, chilled.
- Blanch the beans. Cool, under running cold water, drain, store in airtight container, chilled.
- Make the salad dressings.
- Make the chocolate creams. Cover each, or the trayful, with cling film.
- Prepare first steps for the trifles.

THE DAY BEFORE

- Thaw the pastry for the koulibiacs.
- Roast the ducks. Cover and keep cool (chilled if the weather is hot).
- Slice the tomatoes.
- Soften butter for spreading rolls. Leave at room temperature, covered.
- Make coffee. Store, sealed with cling film in plastic or china or glass jars or jugs.
- In the early evening make up the koulibiacs ready for baking.

THE DAY ITSELF – EARLY

- Take each dish from buffet table as needed, fill, decorate and replace under the cloth. If it's a hot day, lightly spray the cover with cold water. Keep pets well out of the way.
- Bake the koulibiacs, cool, transfer to serving dishes.
- Make the canapés.
- Finish, dress and garnish the salads.
- Decorate the sweets.
- Split, butter and arrange the bread rolls.
- Fill cream jugs for coffee.
- Fill sugar basins.

SCENE-SETTING

FLOWERS AND CANDLELIGHT

Anyone who has ever watched those television series where I was in charge of cookery, kitchen and particularly table settings – *Upstairs, Downstairs, The Duchess of Duke Street, By The Sword Divided* – will have a good idea that flowers play a very important part in my scheme of things when entertaining, but in a particular way.

Of course, in those period dramas I was working with well-documented evidence as to how things were in Britain, and London in particular, in those times. Thus there were hoops of blooms soaring upwards over the vast tables in the Victorian and Edwardian houses of Lord and Lady Bellamy or Louisa Trotter (alias Rosa Lewis), or dried arrangements, plants and even trees, and vast bowls of scented pot-pourri were liberally distributed every-where in the Great Halls of the baronial houses of the 17th century Lacy family.

In another area, on BBC's *Pebble-Mill-at One* over the past years, particularly at Christmas, I have always liked to show the style of arrangement I might use in my own home. Many of these ideas have a strong American influence, for I am a frequent visitor to the United States, where on its Eastern Seaboard they follow a strong traditional style in their decorating. The Christmas tree always provides a good opportunity to experiment with new decoration and I believe I was one of the first, when I demonstrated the effect on *Pebble-Mill*, to use an arrange-ment of silk taffeta bows in clashing pinks, reds, fuschias and oranges on my tree. Used much more widely now, the bows are a simple and attractive way of making things pretty, particularly when used to garland a specific dish on a buffet table.

Other table decorations, for buffets or party tables, are gleaned straight from 18th century England, when the use of flower arrangements actually *on* the table was un-known, but where bays, lemon and orange trees, standard roses and other graphic flora, even fruiting pineapple plants were brought into the dining room from the hot-houses and where pyramids of fruits and dried flower-heads were intricately built to give a feeling of opulence and grandeur to a room.

Today, I am a devotee and advocater of the 'David Hicks' arrangements. I use glass tanks, both vast and miniature, of massed flowers of one kind, giving blocks of colour, which can be placed strategically in sitting or dining room and can be positioned on the floor, console, sill or table with the all-essential spotlight to give an extra all-important dimension.

Dare I say it? I have no time for the rigid 'Hogarth curve' and 'drip triangle' type of flower arrangement. I find them rigid and unfriendly, contrived if not downright awkward in their efforts to embellish a room. For me flowers are for *decorating* not for 'arranging'.

In the summer, if you come to my home, you will see a glass tank of two dozen mixed blue spires of delphiniums on the sitting room floor – spot-lit at night of course – or my hearth will be filled with pots of rubrum or Longiflorum lillies. I don't mind that heavenly scent they exude in the early evening. I find natural flower scents no more overpowering to food than the clashing perfumes, colognes and after-shaves of my guests! A handsome silver sauce tureen of vividly-coloured buttercups or white daisies might be on my table, and a crystal salt-cellar of miniature roses, give me greater pleasure than a cushion of pink carnations and matching plastic bows.

Candles play a major role in my scheme of things, again not singly but masses of them, and not necessarily on the table but in groups of five or six strategically placed in two or three different areas. The candles in each group should not be too close together, otherwise they will melt each other. Electric light is kept to a minimum: a subtle wash from a downlighter here, a clever glow across a wall from an uplighter there. Picture lights if you have them, are perhaps the most useful lighting you can have to give that added subtle punch to a room. Wire them to a dimmer in order to help you balance your effect.

Church candles are the best to use, because of their high beeswax content. They never clash, they don't drip (unless there is a draught), they are long-lasting (though more costly) and somehow it never looks as though you're using up the candles from a previous occasion! I leave them in their sticks and sconces when not in use as I find even un-lit ones give a feeling that a room is lived in.

I am guided by just two unbreakable rules when using candles; the lighting in the sitting room should be only a degree or two brighter than elsewhere in the house and I *never* have candles on the table at lunch time.

TABLE SETTING

I have two guiding principles when it comes to setting the table. The first is to introduce an element of surprise and the second is to use an under-plate.

In the days of vast dinner services, when for grand occasions up to forty items might be set for each guest, the overall effect was gained by the sheer grandeur of the tableware. Nowadays, individual surprises can be achieved by your own personal and very individual mingling of single treasured pieces.

Tableware does not have to be identical as long as it blends. I would suggest that when contemplating the purchase of a dinner service, you choose as the main feature a set of eight decorated dinner plates to blend with your dining room colour scheme.

For other items, plain white or cream china will always fit in or you can echo the colour, texture and/or shape of the main set for a co-ordinated rather than full-matching dinner service. On this basis you will find that carefully selected antique items can be made to work very well with modern pieces.

The size of the items you select is also all-important and this is where the under-plate comes into its own. As the traditional dinner service has reduced in the number of items it contains, so it has also diminished in the size of the pieces themselves. However, use the modern small plate as the receptacle for the food, stand this on a larger plate and

place the pair on a yet larger plate with a folded napkin in between and you have an instantly spectacular effect. Ensure though that the top plate is the right size for the food it contains, so that your efforts are not lost in the middle of an expanse of china or, conversely, that the top plate does not overflow and spoil the effect of the decoration-only under-plates.

White double damask tablecloths with matching napkins impart an elegantly traditional, formal atmosphere to your dining table. But this may not necessarily work with either the occasion or your dining room decor. In which case, choose something softer as a complement to your dinner service: you may even consider dyeing the damask if you have such a thing in your bottom drawer.

Setting the table with these principles in mind may take more time and care but I myself think it is time well spent. for it does mean that you achieve a truly personal effect.

GLASSES

There is an excellent choice of well-designed glass and china about at a price which isn't daunting and where the odd broken or chipped piece can be replaced without an eternal wait. At the other end of the market, there are those elegant specialist shops, where in a rash moment we can buy an heirloom-to-be-used.

Let us assume that you are starting from scratch and give you a basic range for your needs.

Never buy heavily-cut glass unless it is from one of the top glass manufacturers. Real cut glass is made of lead crystal and has a dazzling sparkle as it catches the candlelight. The idea of cutting glass was thought up before the advent of gas and electricity and was designed to add lustre to the atmosphere and enhance the look of the

wine, which was not as clear and bright as it is today. Cheap 'cut' glass is a very different thing.

Buy a dozen at a time.

Buy plain glass – it always looks elegant, even when of an inexpensive make.

Select a voluminous glass. This gives an immediate feel of generosity and welcome. Also one feels drawn to handle a well-shaped bowl of a rounded 10 ounce goblet, cupping and hugging it in a cosy sort of way, and your nose can really get down to sniffing the aroma, whereas you look a bit of an idiot trying to do any of these things with a 4 ounce affair!

Tall stems are elegant, as well as necessary for keeping warm hands away from a cool wine.

If needs must, you could set one glass for all wines, in which case choose the 8 ounce tulip glass.

If you like to have a variety, and why not, then you will need these shapes for table use:

One tall, smaller-bowled, long-stemmed glass for German and Alsatian (and, these days, English) wines; one voluptuous, round-bowled, stemmed glass for other white wines and red wines. (There used to be a difference between a claret glass and a Burgundy glass, which was simply a matter that each region of France produced a glass for its own wine – no more than that.)

One for Champagne and other sparkling wines, which today is the tall, slender, elegant flute. The saucer-shaped bowls are quite acceptable, but the bubble can escape more readily from the larger surface area. Not that complaints were ever heard on that count when the saucer was fashionable.

Glasses for pre-dinner drinks can be tall or squat; I prefer mine to be a straight-sided, heavy-based 10 fluid ounce squat glass. Whisky tots – whisky glasses, that is – are for the Scots and other purists who take their single blend malts seriously.

Sherry can, of course, be served in the traditional (to us in England that is) sherry glass, because you will no doubt have a lot of these in your glass cupboard. If not, then select a larger 5–6 ounce glass on a medium long stem.

The Spanish Copita is not for the British. To use this glass effectively, you have to have great style, flair and aplomb! As a general rule we are much too restrained and inhibited for this.

The liqueur glass, wherever it came from, is of little use to anybody. The most elegant way, and therefore the best way, of serving liqueurs, brandies and eaux-de-vie drinks is in a *small* balloon glass or 'sniffer'. This way you will be rewarded by the aromas which collect in the mouth of the glass to be inhaled for your pleasure.

Cocktail glasses are invariably V-shaped and long stemmed. They should not be too small. They can be as outrageous as you choose: red, green, yellow stems and frosted bowls, coloured rims and all, for the cocktail is a jazzed-up affair, open-minded and whimsical and the glass should match.

A vintage port will be decanted for obvious reasons. I suggest you serve port, Madeira or Marsala as you do sherry, in a slightly larger glass than the traditional port glass, half filled.

DECANTER AND WINE JUGS

Any red wine is improved by decanting, so do use them.

There is no reason at all why a dessert wine should not be decanted and chilled until ready to use.

GLASS HIRE FOR LARGE PARTIES

Most wine merchants will loan glass for parties free of charge. Check that they are in a clean state.

When storing glass at home, your cheap party glasses can be kept in their cartons in garage, loft or cellar.

Best glass should be stored on paper-lined shelves grouped in sizes and rows, ideally not having one size behind another, but ranging the sizes in deep rows from left to right. Store glasses *mouth upwards* keeping dust out of the bowls by laying a paper loosely across the top. Keeping them upside down is asking for the glasses to taste of whatever you last washed the cupboard with.

ARRANGING GLASS ON THE DINNER TABLE

The first glass to be used will be placed at the right-hand top corner of your place setting, the second glass behind it and a third, if called for, behind and in to the left somewhat.

Brandy, port, liqueurs glasses can be on the table to save you having to fetch and carry, or can be left at the ready on a tray on a side table.

Decanters can be on the table. Back-up bottles, corks drawn, are left on a side table. Always have an old but clean and folded linen or cotton napkin at the ready to mop up

LEFT TO RIGHT: Tall glasses for long cool drinks; Champagne flutes; Squat glasses for spirits; Wine glasses

wayward drips. Never wrap a bottle. This is something reserved for restaurants. Hold the bottle in one hand, the folded napkin in the other.

Soda water is the best neutralizer for spilt red wine. Salt 'fixes' the colour, so watch out for this misused technique. Soda water also loosens ice cubes which are frozen together.

FINGER BOWLS

Finger bowls need be provided only if asparagus, artichokes, lobster, game, fruit or any foods which entail the use of fingers are served. The water should be warm, with a squeeze of lemon juice or a splash of roseflower water added. Floating flower heads are a nicety. A clean napkin should be offered *after* your guests have used the one already supplied.

If I have been serving lobsters or crab entailing the use of picks, hammers and crackers, I keep a set of white facecloths specifically for the purpose. These I pop into a steamer as we sit at table with the merest drop of cologne on each one. I then line a basket with a dry, white guest towel, lift the hot steaming cloths from the container with a pair of food tongs and wrap them up before taking them into the dining room: a wonderful 'Gosh! factor' culled straight from the East and brought to the West. Guests adore it. Such details are always appreciated.

IMBIBING

PRE-DINNER DRINKING

I have very strong views on this subject, for this is an area where a feeling of meanness can creep in, but can so easily and very effectively be avoided. This is where the Americans have got things exactly right and achieve the reverse effect and at minimal cost. The answer is *ice* – in abundance!

One ice cube in a gin and tonic will not do when entertaining, or for yourself for that matter, either go out and buy a bag of ice and stow it in the freezer, or start building up a stock of ice the week before your party and transfer it to plastic freezer bags in amounts which fill your ice pail, vase, casserole, bowl or whatever you use. This makes for ease of replenishing.

The first long cool drink you offer your guest should have a minimum of 4 ice cubes in it.

Slip into the glass a quarter-inch thick half slice of lemon, deftly squeezed and twisted, before you pour over a double jigger of gin, vodka, whisky or whatever. Add a stubby glass rod or crusher for the drinker to play with.

Medium and Cream sherry are best served at room temperature 18°–21°C (65°–70°F). Amontillado and the drier sherries are pleasant served lightly chilled but this is a matter of personal taste. Fill the chosen glass two-thirds full.

Keep gin, vodka, Vermouth, dry sherries and mixers in the refrigerator door. This way you are halfway to making a perfect drink. You might even consider having a small drinks fridge if you enjoy offering drinks frequently.

In my opinion Twiglets and crisps are *out*. Any hostess who provides these rather than a small canapé or freshly-pickled olives, has her priorities wrong.

AFTER-DINNER DRINKING

I think liqueurs in the late 1980s are better served over crushed ice. This takes away the stickiness. To crush ice, fold ice cubes in a clean tea towel and bash evenly with a rolling pin or hammer.

The affectation of brandy warmers is for restaurants only. Simply cup the glass in the hands and let natural body heat do the job.

Enjoy the game of 'passing the port', but don't take it too seriously! Serve port, Madeira or Marsala *before* coffee. Serve brandies, eaux-de-vie and liqueurs with coffee.

WINE

Whilst there is a deal of snobbery surrounding wine and wine drinking, there is one habit, considered by many a great affectation, which is not that at all. This is the technique of half-filling a decent-sized, round-bowled goblet and inhaling the bouquet. It is more than half the charm of drinking a good wine. To do it, you should arrange the glass to your right in front of you, your arm comfortably half-extended. Hold the base or foot of the stem with your thumb on the left of the stem, first and second fingers to the right of the stem, gripping it firmly and pressing down on the table at the same time. Now,

start making a slow, steady, firm circular movement with the *forearm*, hardly moving the base of the glass at all. The wine will start to swirl round in the glass, coating the sides, thus exposing a greater area of wine to the air. You will soon learn how to control this operation. This same technique applies to *good* white wines, but it does become a bit of a carry-on if you start sniffing and gargling with a local plonk.

There are, however, two cautions. Firstly, V-shaped and square-shaped glasses will spray the wine right across the table, so don't be tempted to try with this type of glass.

Secondly, coating the inside of the mouth with wine by drawing air through your mouthful can be fraught with hazard for first-time triers, but once you are practised at it, it does increase the pleasure of life as each taste-bud gets its turn, so to speak.

WINES WITH THE RECIPES

Whilst I don't hold entirely with the old adage of dry white wines with fish and poultry and red wines with red meats, because, for instance, I enjoy claret with chicken and a light red wine with grilled salmon, it *is* a good guide for a beginner. But do experiment: try drinking a sweet white wine with blue cheese for example, and certainly try a medium sweet wine with smoked fish.

That said, it is also true that what is *dry* is a very subjective affair. What is *sweet* can be, but the areas for differing are less provocative and the options for choice more limited thus diminishing margin for disagreement.

So I have opted to guide you through 'blocks' of wines, listed by type (with areas), with which – give or take the inevitable subjective views – you should be safe.

VERY DRY WHITE WINES
Muscadet, Chablis, Verdicchio and some types of Soave, Peñedes.

MEDIUM DRY WHITE WINES
Blancs Fumés, a dry wine from Orvieto, Soave, Corvo, Frascati, Vinho Verde, some Chablis, dry Vouvrays, Chiantis (these wines can be sweet or dry), White Beaujolais (not easy to find), white Riojas.

FULL-BODIED FRUITY WHITE WINES
Côte d'or and other top class white Burgundies, Chardonnays (particularly those from California), white Rhône wines, Orvieto, Navarre wines.

LIGHT OR 'SOFT' WHITE WINES, MAINLY SUITABLE FOR APERITIF DRINKING
Mosel and Rhein wines (though not the richer late-gathered wines), some Traminers, Liebfraumilch Rieslings, Sylvaners and Tokays (from Alsace).

SPICY WINES
Alsace, but only those made from the Muscat, Traminer or Gewurztraminer grape.

MEDIUM SWEET WHITE WINES
Graves, medium-dry Vouvrays, wines made from the Chenin grape, white Lambrusco.

SWEET WHITE WINES
Sauterne, Barsacs, Sweet Vouvrays, Beaume de Venises, Muscatels, Tokays.

FULL-BODIED RED WINES
Burgundies, Californian wines, Riojas, Barolos, red wines from the Eastern European countries, Rhône wines.

LIGHT BUT FRUITY RED WINES
Beaujolais, Red wines from the Loire, young clarets of a generic type rather than a classified château.

DRY RED WINES
Bordeaux (clarets), Chianti, Valpolicella, Barbaresco.

DRY CHAMPAGNE
Brut, Extra sec.

SWEET OR 'SOFT' CHAMPAGNE
Demi-sec, Rich.

OTHER SPARKLING WINES
Dry: Sekt; Sweet: Asti Spumante and some Spanish Champagne.

THE PARTY'S OVER

WASHING UP ORGANIZATION AND A SENSE OF ORDER

I actually like washing up and am an expert on the subject! Therefore let me list the essentials needed to make this task an easier one for you:

Hot water in abundance – so, turn the thermostat up, or put the immersion heater on *early*.

Detergent – a mild one: have a spare squeezy to hand – you will need a lot!

Strong bin bags (with the necessary straps to tie them) –
(1) to take waste food.
(2) an extra strong one to hold bottles, though if a quantity of wine is consumed, it is better to retain the boxes outside the back door.
(3) one for paper napkins, plates, cartons and the like.

Extra Pedal Bin Liners – to line waste paper baskets, with the necessary straps to tie them when full.

An old tin (such as a paint tin) – to receive safely cigarette ends and ash. (This should be put outside before you retire.)

All available work surfaces cleared – to receive dirty china and glass. Remove everything which can logically be placed elsewhere for a time.

Washing-up machine and sinks empty and at the ready – if you don't have a double sink unit, then arrange to have a large plastic washing-up bowl to act as a rinsing sink.

Large empty containers –
(1) to soak cutlery. This can be a bowl, pan or a heavy duty plastic tub or bucket. Fill it with scalding water and a *cupful* of detergent.
(2) to receive débris from plates and dishes as you scrape each plate. This should be placed at working height to eliminate the need to stoop.

Plenty of dry tea towels
Extra rolls of paper towels
Plastic food containers – for leftovers.

Cling film and food bags – to cover and store left-over foods. This should be done as soon as the dishes are removed from the table by you or your helpers.

Extra Work Surface – If you are having a very large party, it is a good idea to borrow or hire a trestle table or some other suitable table to give extra space, having organized your put-down areas, it is equally important to have a 'ready-to-put-away' area.

Trays – Borrow, or hire, extra large trays. These act as extra work surfaces and are also a means of segregating china, glass, cutlery, ashtrays etc., and can always await their turn in the queue by being placed safely on the floor, under the table, hidden from view.

ORDER OF CLEARING

Tray	Rinsing container or sink
Work surface	Draining and drying
Soaking container	Ready to to put away area
Washing sink	Put away

SOME DO's AND DON'Ts

Do
(i) Wipe any plates which have mayonnaise on them with paper towels and wash separately. Mayonnaise is the kiss of death to washing-up water: it leaves a thin film of grease on everything.
(ii) Segregate dirty china, glass and cutlery.
(iii) Stack pans and bakeware, filled with soapy water where necessary, somewhere safely out of the way until you are ready to tackle them.
(iv) Wash glass in hot soapy water and rinse in *hot* water.
(v) Scrape debris into debris container.
(vi) Put cutlery into cutlery rinse before piling plates ready for washing.
(vii) Grade china in sizes.
(viii) Empty, rinse out and re-fill the sink regularly.
(ix) Drain well before drying.
(x) Stack, and line things up in an orderly fashion.
(xi) Put a drop of washing-up liquid in scalding hot rinsing water.
(xii) Lay a tea towel over the draining surface when washing glass: this protects delicate rims.
(xiii) Take off rings and other jewellery to wash up.
(xiv) Have a tea-towel impregnated with silver cleaner for that final buff-up.
(xv) Stack for putting away, in the same orderly fashion as for clearing.

Don't
(i) Don't stack glasses inside each other.
(ii) Don't carry piles of plates with food and cutlery stacked between them.
(iii) Don't fill your sink with a mixture of china, glass and cutlery.
(iv) Don't 'push' china and glass against each other – this causes rims to be chipped.
(v) Don't wash glass in the same water as china and cutlery – this causes smearing.
(vi) Don't hold a glass by the stem when drying it. Always 'cup' the glass in your hand and avoid any 'twisting' movement: dry 'one way'.

EMERGENCY MEASURES
Have to hand for any party:
(i) Spirit cleaner and a non-fluffy (lint free) cloth to deal quickly with grease splashes
(ii) Brush pan and brush
(iii) Paper towels
(iv) Clean dish cloth
(v) Bottle of soda water for neutralizing red-wine spills
(vi) Clean tea towel to slide under wetted table cloth to protect a polished surface
(vii) Carafe of water and aspirin
All these should be collected together in a box and placed at the ready where you and one other know where it is.

DOWN TO BASICS

LINING TART TINS

All tins, whether plain or non-stick, should be brushed with clarified butter, then chilled for a minute or two to set the butter, before lining with pastry. This grips the pastry.

Small tarts and barquettes can be made with raw pastry, i.e. not baked blind, if you prefer. In which case allow 2 minutes or so longer cooking time. This will mean that a custard filling will have a firmer set. That said, you do get a crisper crust and lighter-textured filling if you do bake them blind first. And, of course, pastry shells can be baked in advance and stored in an airtight tin, in layers well-cushioned with soft paper.

To finish the baking, stand the tarts carefully on a baking sheet and use a good pouring jug or a small, 25 ml (1 fl oz) ladle with a spout to fill with the liquid.

Depending how thin or thick you roll pastry (I have taken a medium line), 225 g (8 oz) shortcrust (or puff) pastry will line:
(a) 24 mini tartlet tins, 5 cm (2 inches) in diameter, 2 cm ($\frac{3}{4}$ inch) deep
(b) 12 barquette tins, 11 cm ($4\frac{1}{2}$ inches) long × 5 cm (2 inches) wide
(c) 12 ordinary tart tins, 6 cm ($2\frac{1}{2}$ inches) in diameter, 2.5 cm (1 inch) deep
(d) 6 large individual tart tins, 10 cm (4 inches) in diameter, 3 cm ($1\frac{1}{8}$ inches) deep
(e) 8 large individual tart tins 7.5 cm (3 inches) in diameter, 2.5 cm (1 inch) deep

A savoury or sweet custard made with 3 small eggs and 300 ml ($\frac{1}{2}$ pint) milk or cream will fill:
36 of (a); 18 of (b); 18 of (c); 4 of (d); 6 of (e). This excludes any other ingredients, such as prawns, diced meats, fish, mushrooms. In which case it will fill slightly more cases.

RICH SHORTCRUST PASTRY

MAKES 225 g (8 oz)

150 g (5 oz) plain white flour
$\frac{1}{2}$ teaspoon salt
75 g (3 oz) unsalted butter, cut into small cubes
15 g ($\frac{1}{2}$ oz) lard, cut into cubes
1 egg yolk, beaten mixed with 1 teaspoon water

PREPARATION TIME: 15 minutes, plus chilling
COOKING TIME: 10–15 minutes
OVEN: 220°C, 425°F, Gas Mark 7

1 Sieve the flour with the salt into a basin. Make a well and put in the butter, lard and beaten egg. Peck and pinch the mixture together, gradually incorporating the flour from the sides of the well so that it eventually forms a dough. Knead lightly and form into a square in a floured plastic bag. Chill for 1 hour or more.

2 Roll out the pastry on a lightly floured board. Cut to fit the tins being used. Line the tins and bake in a preheated oven for 10–15 minutes until crisp and golden.

PUFF PASTRY

MAKES 450 g (1 lb)

225 g (8 oz) plain flour
1 teaspoon salt
225 g (8 oz) butter
about 6 tablespoons water
1 tablespoon lemon juice

PREPARATION TIME: about 1 hour, plus chilling

1 Mix the flour and salt. Soften the butter on a plate with a palette knife, then rub 2 tablespoons of it into the flour. Add the water and lemon juice and mix to a soft, pliable dough. Knead on a floured board until smooth.

2 Shape the remaining butter into an oblong 15 × 7.5 cm (6 × 3 inches). Roll the pastry into a 15 cm (6 inch) square. Place the butter on one side and fold over the pastry to enclose it. Press the edges to seal.

3 Turn the pastry, so that the fold is to the side, then roll out to a rectangle 13 × 39 cm (5 × 15 inches). Fold the bottom third up and the top third down and seal the edges, pressing lightly with the rolling pin. Slip into a plastic bag and chill for 20 minutes. Place the pastry with the fold to one side and repeat the above sequence, including the chilling. Repeat 5 times more. After the final chilling, shape the pastry as required.

COOKING PASTA

Shops today are full of every sort, shape and size of pasta, both dry, *Pasta Secca*, or fresh, *Pasta all'uovo*. with subdivisions of *Pasta Corta*, which is all those little shapes – alphabets, shells, snails, bows, propellers, umbrellas, wheels et al. These are mostly used for garnishes, though shells are ideal for cold pasta salads as their cavities hold plenty of juicy dressing.

Pasta Asciutta includes all the long types: *spaghetti*, *maccheróne* (It's only in Naples where the Italians call it *macaroni*), *lasagne*, *lumache*, *zita*, *rigatoni*. All of which need oil, butter or a sauce or both and freshly grated Parmesan cheese.

Angolotti ravioli and *cannelloni* are the types which are served stuffed before being coated with a sauce.

Pasta is extremely simple to cook, the only problem being that you need a really big pan. There are a few basic rules:

1 You need an abundance of water: for 8 people, allowing a good 100 g (4 oz) of dry pasta per head, you need 9 litres (2 gallons) of boiling water.

2 Add the salt to the boiling water just before adding the pasta.

3 Add a slurp of cooking oil, to help keep the strands or sheets separate.

4 Add the pasta, a little at a time, so that the water doesn't go off the boil. With long pasta, lower it gently into the water, letting it bend round as it softens. Some cooks like to break their pasta into manageable lengths, around 15–20 cm (6–8 inches). To break, fold the long *uncooked* spaghetti in a clean towel, then pull down over the edge of a table to break into shorter lengths.

5 No exact cooking time can be given as pastas vary so much in thickness. Follow the instructions on the packet, but the golden Italian rule that all pasta be cooked *al dente* applies (still biteable and resistant to the tooth). So keep lifting a bit out of the pan and testing it after, say, 10 minutes. (Home-made pasta rarely takes longer than 5–7 minutes.)

6 When the pasta is cooked, tip the whole lot into a large colander or sieve to drain.

Now comes the Smith method. I now wash away any surplus starch by running scalding water over the pasta, then drain it again, before tossing and bathing it in butter or a mixture of butter and olive oil. Good butter and olive or arachid oil are essential. Either eat it plain or top with one of the sauces on pages 114–117. Dredge with the all-essential Parmesan (or the stronger-flavoured Pecorino).

If you really cannot get fresh Parmesan or Pecorino, then I suggest using mature Gruyère. Never Cheddar or Cheshire, Edam or Gouda.

If you are cooking pasta shells or other shapes, then extra care must be taken to ensure that all the water has been drained away. The shells are designed to hold sauces and dressings, therefore they also hold water.

TO COOK IN ADVANCE

1 Cook your pasta to the degree of softness you prefer. Rinse it in a sieve or colander under running cold water to get rid of all the starch: leave it to drain, for 10 minutes or so, shaking it well. mop away excess water with paper towels. Tip into a large strong plastic bag. Pour in 2–3 tablespoons of olive oil and shake to coat.

2 There are 2 ways of reheating pasta. Either plunge it into a large pan of boiling water for a minute or so, draining it after it is hot through; or, melt a little butter with an equal amount of oil in a large non-stick pan, tip the pasta, and, using 2 dinner forks, or a wooden pasta fork (for which purpose they are made) fork the pasta around in a sort of 'up' (from the bottom and at the sides) over and drop. Don't try to mix it round.

BASIC PIZZA DOUGH

450 g (1 lb) plain white flour
2 teaspoons baking powder
1 teaspoon salt
75 g (3 oz) butter, hard, cubed
300 ml ($\frac{1}{2}$ pint) buttermilk or single cream

PREPARATION TIME: 30 minutes

1 Sieve the flour, baking powder and salt into a baking bowl. Rub in the butter with the finger tips until you have sand-like texture.

2 With a fork, mix in enough buttermilk or cream to form a firmish dough. Knead the dough on a floured surface until smooth. Form into 2 'sausages' about 6 cm (2$\frac{1}{2}$ inches) diameter.

3 Cut into 20–30 pieces. Roll into balls, then lightly roll with a floured rolling pin into 6 cm (2$\frac{1}{2}$ inch) rounds.

SUCCESSFUL BREADMAKING

There is nothing more mouth-watering than the smell of freshly baked bread. To achieve a result which tastes and looks as good as it smells, there are a few points to remember.

THE INGREDIENTS

Yeast is the agent which makes the bread rise and can be bought both fresh – usually from a local bakery – or dried in individual sachets in the supermarkets.

Fresh yeast should be a creamy colour, smell sweet and crumble between the fingers easily. It will keep in an airtight plastic bag in the refrigerator for up to one month. It keeps in the freezer for the same length of time. If freezing yeast, weigh in recipe sized portions before freezing and thaw for 30 minutes at room temperature before using.

Fresh yeast can be added to the flour by three methods. The basic method is to blend it first with warm liquid, then add to the flour. Secondly, there is the batter method in which one third of the flour is mixed with the yeast liquid, left in a warm place for 20 minutes until frothy, then added to the rest of the flour, etc. Finally, the yeast can be blended with part of the liquid, then added to the dry ingredients and the remaining liquid added.

Dried yeast is just as good as fresh and often more easily obtainable. It will keep in an airtight container (or in its foil sachets) for 6 months. Dried yeast needs sugar and liquid to activate it. It is more concentrated than fresh yeast, so generally only half as much is needed.

Using the correct flour is essential in breadmaking. 'Strong' flours have a high gluten content which helps in the raising of the bread, making it lighter with a more open

texture. Using brown flour gives a closer texture and a stronger, more distinctive flavour. There are many different flours now on the market as well as white and wholemeal – wheatmeal, stone ground, granary and rye.

Salt improves the flavour and also affects the gluten in the flour. Too much kills the yeast making the bread heavy and uneven, whilst too little makes the dough rise too quickly – accurate measuring is very important.

The liquid can be water, which gives an even texture and crisp crust most suitable for plain breads; or milk and water or milk alone, which will give a softer texture and the bread will stay softer and fresher longer. The amount of liquid can depend on the absorbency of the flour and needs to be hand-hot to quicken up the process.

The fat can be lard, butter, margarine or oil and makes the dough softer. Plain mixtures rise faster than the richer ones that contain fat, sugar, fruit and eggs.

THE METHOD

If the ingredients and utensils are warm rather than chilled, the process is speeded up somewhat.

Measure the ingredients carefully.

Kneading the dough is essential as it strengthens the gluten in the flour, helping to give elasticity to the dough and a better chance to rise well and evenly. Knead for a good 10 minutes, until the dough is firm, smooth and no longer sticky.

The dough needs to rise in a warm place in a greased or oiled plastic bag to prevent a skin forming. Extreme heat kills the yeast. Extreme cold retards its growth, so the dough can be left to rise in a refrigerator overnight or for up to 24 hours. The risen dough should spring back when pressed gently with a floured finger.

The second kneading is known as 'knocking back' and gives the dough a good texture. Knead for 2–3 minutes to knock out any air bubbles.

Shape and leave in the tins or baking sheets, which should be well greased. Only half fill tins to allow for rising, cover with oiled plastic and allow to rise a second time. This second rising stage is called 'proving' and is always done in a warm temperature until the dough rises to the top of the tins or has doubled in size. To keep the top loaves flat for making neat sandwiches, cover a baking sheet with lightly oiled foil. Place on top of the dough in the tins before the second rising, oiled side down. Place ovenproof weights on top and bake as usual.

Glaze and bake in a preheated very hot oven, so that the extreme heat will kill the yeast. When the cooking time is up, turn the loaves out of the tins and tap the bottom, a hollow sound indicates that the bread is cooked. If still soft and doughy, return to the oven without the tins, upside down, for a further 10 minutes.

The bread needs to be cooled on a wire tray, so that air can circulate around it, otherwise any remaining moisture will make the crisp crust go soft.

Bread is best eaten fresh, especially brown bread, but it can be refreshed in the oven by wrapping the bread in foil and reheating at 230°C, 450°F, Gas Mark 8 for 5–10 minutes, letting the bread cool before removing the foil. For a more crusty loaf, reheat without foil.

WHITE BREAD

MAKES one 1 kg (2 lb) loaf and one 450 g (1 lb) loaf or 18 rolls

1 tablespoon dried or 15 g ($\frac{1}{2}$ oz) fresh yeast
$\frac{1}{4}$ teaspoon sugar
450 ml ($\frac{3}{4}$ pint) warm water
700 g (1$\frac{1}{2}$ lb) strong plain flour
2 teaspoons salt
1 teaspoon lard

GLAZE:
2 teaspoons salt and 2 tablespoons water or *beaten egg and milk*

PREPARATION TIME: 30 minutes, plus proving
COOKING TIME: 35–45 minutes
OVEN: 230°C, 450°F, Gas Mark 8

This basic white bread dough could also be shaped into individual rolls, knots, plaits, etc. Sprinkle the rolls with sesame or poppy seeds or glaze with egg for a shiny top, salt water for a crusty finish, or dust with flour for a soft roll.

1 Grease a 1 kg (2 lb) and a 450 g (1 lb) loaf tin. Mix the yeast, sugar and water together in a small bowl and leave in a warm place for 10 minutes until frothy.

2 Sift the flour and salt into a large bowl and rub in the lard with the fingertips.

3 Add the yeast liquid and blend together until a firm dough is formed and the sides of the bowl are clean. Turn out on to a lightly floured work surface and knead for about 10 minutes or until the dough is smooth, glossy and elastic. Place the dough in a large oiled plastic bag and leave in a warm place for 1$\frac{1}{2}$ hours, or until double in volume.

4 Knock back and knead again for 2–3 minutes to knock out any air bubbles. Cut into 2 pieces, one twice the size of the other. Shape to fit the tins and place inside. Place the filled tins back into the oiled plastic bag(s) and leave to rise again in a warm place for 30–40 minutes, or until the dough has risen to the top of the tins.

5 For a crusty top, brush with the salt dissolved in the water. For a shiny top, brush with beaten egg and milk.

6 Bake in a preheated oven for 35–40 minutes. The loaves are cooked when you tap the bottom of the unmoulded loaf and it sounds hollow. For a really crusty loaf, return the unmoulded loaves to the oven on a baking tray for a further 5 minutes. Cool on a wire tray. F

F Freeze for up to 6 weeks. Thaw for 2–3 hours at room temperature.

WHOLEMEAL BREAD

MAKES two 1 kg (2 lb) loaves or four 450 g (1 lb) loaves

25 g (1 oz) dried or 50 g (2 oz) fresh yeast
1 teaspoon sugar
900 ml (1¼ pints) warm water
1.5 kg (3 lb) wholemeal flour
2 tablespoons caster sugar
2 tablespoons salt
50 g (2 oz) lard

PREPARATION TIME: 30 minutes, plus proving
COOKING TIME: 35–40 minutes
OVEN: 230°C, 450°F, Gas Mark 8

1 Grease two 1 kg (2 lb) loaf tins. Mix the yeast and sugar with 1 cup of the measured warm water in a small bowl and leave it in a warm place for about 10 minutes until it is frothy.

2 Sift the flour, caster sugar and salt into a large bowl, then rub in the lard with the fingertips.

3 Pour in the yeast liquid and the remaining water and mix to form a firm dough. Turn out on to a lightly floured work surface and knead with the heel of the hand for 10 minutes. Place in a large, oiled plastic bag and leave in a warm place for 1–1½ hours, until doubled in volume.

4 Knock back and knead again for 5 minutes. Divide the dough into the desired sizes and place in the prepared loaf tins. Return to the oiled plastic bag and leave in a warm place until the dough almost rises to the tops of the tins.

5 For a crusty top, brush with salted water (sprinkling cracked wheat on the top looks attractive).

6 Bake in a preheated oven for 35–40 minutes, until completely cooked. To test, knock the base of the baked loaf with the knuckle, it should sound hollow! Turn out on to a wire tray to cool. [F]

[F] Freeze for up to 6 weeks. Thaw for 3–4 hours at room temperature.

BREAD FINISHES

For a crusty top, brush before baking with 2 teaspoons of salt dissolved in 2 tablespoons water.

For a soft, shiny crust, brush before baking with beaten egg or egg and milk.

For a floury crust, lightly sift a little flour over the top before baking.

For a sticky, shiny glaze use either honey, golden syrup or sugar water: dissolve 2 tablespoons sugar in 2 tablespoons water. Brush over the cooked, warm loaf.

For extra crunch, sprinkle before baking with sesame, poppy, caraway, celery or fennel seeds.

BRIDGE ROLLS

MAKES 18

1 tablespoon dried or 15 g (½ oz) fresh yeast
¼ teaspoon caster sugar
85 ml (3 fl oz) warm milk
225 g (8 oz) strong white flour
1 teaspoon salt
50 g (2 oz) butter
1 egg
beaten egg (optional) to glaze

PREPARATION TIME: 30 minutes, plus proving
COOKING TIME: about 20 minutes
OVEN: 220°C, 425°F, Gas Mark 7

I have never had a hand in Bridge (if you'll forgive the pun) but for those enthusiasts who have, the Bridge Roll was invented! So loath are these card players to leave their velvet-covered tables (as with the Earl of Sandwich at the gaming tables), that a device in the form of a miniscule soft, semi-sweet bread roll was thought up to contain their favourite sandwich fillings and assuage any hunger pangs.

1 Grease a baking sheet. Mix the yeast and sugar with the milk and leave in a warm place for about 10 minutes until frothy.

2 Sift the flour and salt into a large bowl and rub in the butter with the fingertips.

3 Add the yeast mixture with the egg and mix to form a soft dough. Turn on to a lightly floured work surface and knead for 10 minutes or until smooth. Place in an oiled plastic bag and leave in a warm place for 1½–2 hours until the dough has doubled in volume.

4 Knock back and knead again for 5 minutes, then cut into 18 equal pieces. Shape each into a roll about 7.5 cm (3 inches) long. Place fairly close together in rows on the prepared baking sheet. Slip the tray into the oiled plastic bag and leave to rise in a warm place for a further 20–30 minutes, until almost doubled in size.

5 For a glazed shiny top, brush now with a little beaten egg. Bake in a preheated oven for about 20 minutes. Cool on a wire tray. Ⓕ

Ⓕ Freeze for 1 month. Thaw at room temperature for 1–2 hours.

BASIC RICH BROWN BEEF STOCK

MAKES 4 PINTS

1.5 kg (3 lb) mixed marrowbones and others, sawn into manageable pieces
1.5 kg (3 lb) shin of beef, trimmed of all fat, cut into 5 cm (2 inch) pieces
2 tablespoons olive or soy oil
225 g (8 oz) carrot, peeled and sliced
2 sticks celery, trimmed and sliced
1 leek, trimmed and roughly chopped
100 g (4 oz) field or flat-cap mushrooms
600 ml (1 pint) Burgundy-type red wine
a fresh bouquet garni or 2 commercial sachets
450 g (1 lb) tomatoes, skinned, seeded and chopped
1 teaspoon salt
1 tablespoon black peppercorns
2.75–3.5 litres (5–6 pints) cold water
1 × 100 g (4 oz) onion, peeled and cut in half

PREPARATION TIME: 30 minutes
COOKING TIME: 3½–3¾ hours
OVEN: 240°C, 475°F, Gas Mark 9

1 Place the bones in a roasting tin and brown in the preheated oven, turning them with tongs to ensure they are well coloured. This can take 45 minutes to 1 hour.

2 Remove the bones and place on one side on a tray. Transfer the roasting tin to the top of the cooker and brown the shin in the residue fats on all sides, over a fierce heat, working with a manageable batch at a time.

3 Heat the oil in a soup pan until smoking. Add the carrots and celery and brown over a high heat, stirring to ensure even colouring and no burning. Lower the heat to almost minimal. Add the bones, meat and all the other ingredients apart from the onion, pouring in sufficient cold water to cover. (Discard any fatty residues.)

4 Bring to the boil very slowly in order to extract all the goodness from the bones and meat.

5 Meanwhile, brown the onion. Place the halves, cut-side down, in a dry frying pan over a low heat, or on top of an Aga hotplate. Allow them to brown gently but completely. They should be caramelized but not burnt.

6 Once the stock is boiling, add the browned onion and keep at a steady boil, not just simmering. Be careful, however, as a rapid boil will cloud the stock. Cook, uncovered, for 3 hours, skimming off any scum which rises to the surface during this lengthy process.

7 Cool. Decant the stock through a lined sieve as for the Basic Chicken Stock (see page 22). Cool completely, then chill overnight. Ⓐ Ⓕ

BASIC CHICKEN STOCK

1 tablespoon butter or soy oil
100 g (4 oz) carrot, peeled and sliced
2 large leeks (white part only), trimmed, washed and finely sliced
2 stalks celery, trimmed and sliced
1 × 1.5 kg (3 lb) chicken (or boiling fowl)
750 g–1 kg (1½–2 lb) knuckle of veal, chopped into manageable pieces
100 g (4 oz) white-cap mushrooms, rubbed clean and sliced
1 bouquet garni sachet
600 ml (1 pint) dry white wine
1.75 litres (3 pints) or more cold water
2 teaspoons salt
12 white peppercorns

PREPARATION TIME: 30 minutes
COOKING TIME: 2½ hours

1 Melt the butter in a large pan without browning it. Add the carrots, leeks and celery, cover and soften over a low heat, without browning, for 12–15 minutes.

2 Add the chicken, knuckle pieces, mushrooms and bouquet garni. Pour the wine and water over to cover. Add the salt and peppercorns, then bring to the boil *slowly*. Adjust the heat, so that the liquid is boiling, but only gently so. Rapid boiling creates a cloudy stock.

3 Boil at this gentle pace for 2 hours, taking the chicken out after 1½ hours and skimming the surface of any scum which may collect.

4 Cool, then decant the clear stock into a large bowl through a sieve lined with clean muslin or paper towel. Be patient, let the stock trickle through at its own pace: do not be tempted to press it through. Change the paper, or rinse the muslin from time to time to rid it of any sediments.

5 Chill until ready for use. Ⓐ Ⓕ

Ⓐ The stock will keep for 3–5 days in a refrigerator.
Ⓕ The stock can be frozen for up to 6 months. Freeze in several batches for ease of use.

Note:
Use up the chicken or boiling fowl in a mayonnaise, or in a chicken and pasta salad. It will curry well, too.

RICH CHICKEN STOCK

1 × 1.75 kg (4 lb) fresh chicken
1 knuckle of veal, washed and cut up
4 sticks celery
1 medium onion, peeled and quartered
1 small head fennel, cleaned and quartered
2 medium carrots, peeled and sliced
2 garlic cloves, peeled
2 bouquet garni sachets
2 teaspoons whole white peppercorns
600 ml (1 pint) dry white wine
2.25 litres (4 pints) cold water

PREPARATION TIME: 30 minutes
COOKING TIME: 1¾–2 hours

1 Put the chicken and veal knuckle into a large pan. Pack all the other ingredients round, then cover with the wine and cold water. Bring to the boil slowly, to extract all the flavours, then simmer for 1¼–1½ hours.

2 Remove the chicken. Continue boiling the stock for a further 20 minutes.

3 Strain through a lined sieve as for the Basic Chicken Stock. Chicken stock can 'turn' quickly so stand the pan of strained stock in a sink with cold water running around it, and stir the stock for even cooling. When it is cool, skim off all the fats and refrigerate. Ⓐ Ⓕ

vigorously. Beat this well in before adding the next few drops. It is essential to take care in the early stages of mayonnaise making – if you are meticulous at the beginning, you will have no trouble later.

3 After the first tablespoonful or so has been added slowly, you can start to add the oil more quickly – experience will teach you just when this can be done. As soon as the emulsion starts to reject the oil (this is quite different from curdling) add a little vinegar and beat until it is creamy again. Mayonnaise is curdled when the solid part goes thin and flecky. If this happens, you must start again with a single egg yolk and work the curdled mayonnaise into it drop by drop. Sometimes a tablespoon of boiling water added to the curdled mayonnaise works.

4 Keep the mayonnaise as stiff as your arm will allow! By this I mean that if you have a strong arm you will be able to have mayonnaise as thick as butter, which can virtually be cut with a knife. When a more liquid mayonnaise is needed, thin down with single cream, vinegar or cold water (or a combination of all three); water gives a blander result than vinegar, cream adds richness. Ⓐ

Ⓐ Mayonnaise does not keep indefinitely, just 4–5 days. Store in a cool, but not cold, place. If it begins to look oily, add a spoonful of boiling water and whisk until creamy again.

VARIATIONS

The finished mayonnaise can be flavoured with ketchup, sherry, lemon juice, brandy, Worcestershire sauce etc. When next using mayonnaise to make Tartare Sauce, add a few chopped raw gooseberries for a sauce with 'kick'.

4 Skin and bone the chicken, then cut the meat into bite-sized striplets. Refrigerate, covered with cling film, for use in another dish.

Ⓐ The stock will keep for 3–5 days in a refrigerator.
Ⓕ Freeze for up to 6 months.

MAYONNAISE

MAKES 1½ PINTS

6 egg yolks
salt
freshly ground white pepper
1 teaspoon dry mustard
600 ml (1 pint) oil (half soy oil, half olive oil) at room temperature
2 tablespoons wine vinegar

PREPARATION TIME: 15 minutes

1 Put the yolks into a round-bottomed basin. This is essential as you need to collect and control the yolks within a small area. Add the salt, mustard and a little pepper and work these with a balloon whisk, until they are really thick and sticky.

2 Have the oil in a jug, then, using a teaspoon, add the first few drops of oil to the egg mixture, whisking

BASIC VINAIGRETTE SAUCE

MAKES 200 ml (⅓ pint)

6 tablespoons olive oil
½ teaspoon Dijon mustard
2 tablespoons red or white wine vinegar
¼ teaspoon caster sugar
salt
freshly ground black pepper
1 garlic clove, finely chopped (optional)
fresh herbs, eg basil, oregano, parsley, chive, mint (optional)

PREPARATION TIME: 5 minutes

1 Put the oil, mustard, vinegar, caster sugar, salt and pepper into a screw-top jar and shake well to blend. Ⓐ

2 Add the garlic and fresh herbs just before using.

Ⓐ Vinaigrette Sauce keeps almost indefinitely in a screw-top jar, but do not add garlic or herbs until ready for use.

Breakfast

Britain — and the ex-colonies — are the only countries in the world which enjoy a good breakfast. Scandinavia, Holland and Germany come a close second but never quite achieve our full glorious meal of fruit, porridge, crisply grilled rashers of bacon, basted eggs, tomatoes, mushrooms, crunchy fried bread and — if you're from Ulster or the North — a slice of spicy black pudding!; all this 'finished off' with slices of toast dripping with butter and marmalade.

Though our approach to this meal has undergone a change, breakfast, or its later version, brunch, can still be a particularly enjoyable time to entertain, whether you choose a simple or an elaborate menu. Here are ideas for whatever type of breakfast or brunch you fancy; even the luxury of a lazy breakfast in bed with your favourite newspaper.

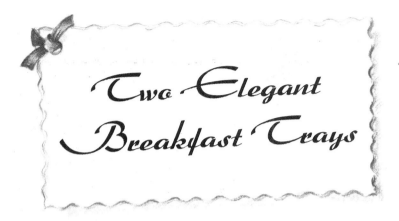

Two Elegant Breakfast Trays

PRUNES IN BLACKCURRANT TEA

GRILLED GAMMON SLICE WITH PARSLEY AND MINT

APPLE AND MUSHROOM COCKTAIL

SHIRRED EGGS WITH PRAWNS AND TOMATOES

As someone who is wide awake, bright-eyed and bushy-tailed at 6 o'clock in the morning, I am hardly the perfect candidate for taking breakfast in bed! I am, however, the best *provider* of this start-to-the-day treat.

There is but one golden rule and that is the size of the tray. It must be large enough to see the operation to its successful conclusion. If you don't possess such a monster size, then I suggest *two* trays is the most manageable way to cope with this elegant off-site hospitality!

One – the first to be delivered to the bedside – should hold all the paraphernalia for tea or coffee, and the chilled fresh fruit juice or whatever astringent starter you have thought up. This should be carefully placed on a bedside table. Fifteen minutes later, two or three pillows or cushions must be placed behind your guest's back to give comfortable support. Another firm pillow has to be put across the lap to receive the *second* tray bearing your deliciously prepared main dish.

Also on this tray will be a side plate, napkin, toast rack, butter dish and knife, marmalade and honey pots with their attendant spoons, knives, forks, mini salt and pepper mill. Leave room, too, for an indulgent magazine and fresh flowers.

Having looked after the all-important provision of food, you could also provide a cassette of some suitable music and, as perfect host or hostess, run a deep, soothing bath for your guest.

PRUNES IN BLACKCURRANT TEA

SERVES 6

1 × 350 g (12 oz) packet giant Agen or California prunes
25 g (1 oz) blackcurrant tea
900 ml (1½ pints) boiling water
25–50 g (1–2 oz) caster sugar (optional)
juice of ½ lemon
½ teaspoon vanilla essence

PREPARATION TIME: 15 minutes, plus infusing and chilling
COOKING TIME: 5 minutes

Blackcurrant tea makes a refreshing drink – in the States it is top of the list for summer drinking – it also adds an excellent dimension to stewed prunes. As prunes keep well under refrigeration or frozen, make up a packet at a time.

1 Put the prunes into a saucepan. Put the tea into a jug or teapot. Pour over the boiling water and allow to infuse for 10–15 minutes. Decant over the prunes and add the sugar, if liked, juice and essence.

2 Simmer over minimal heat until just tender, about 5 minutes. Cool.

3 Pit the prunes carefully, they should not look crushed, then return them to the syrup. Chill well.

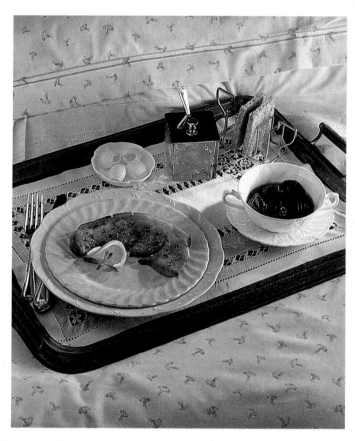

Grilled gammon slice with parsley and mint; Prunes in blackcurrant tea

GRILLED GAMMON SLICE WITH PARSLEY AND MINT

SERVES 1

1 × 175-225 g (6–8 oz) green gammon rasher, 8 mm (⅓ inch) thick
soy oil or butter for brushing
4 mint leaves
1 small sprig parsley
freshly ground black pepper
squeeze lemon juice
lemon twist, to garnish

PREPARATION TIME: 5 minutes
COOKING TIME: 4–6 minutes

1 Preheat the grill to searing hot. Brush the gammon with soy oil or butter on both sides. Grill 10 cm (4 inches) from the heat source for 2–3 minutes each side.

2 Before transferring to a warm plate, sprinkle with the herbs and season well with the pepper. Squeeze over a few drops of lemon juice; add a twist of lemon. You do not need to add salt, most gammon or ham is salty enough.

Apple and mushroom cocktail; Shirred eggs with prawns and tomatoes

APPLE AND MUSHROOM COCKTAIL

· SERVES 1

juice of ½ large lemon
¼ teaspoon mild French mustard
salt
freshly ground black pepper
¼ teaspoon caster sugar (optional)
2 teaspoons good olive oil or grapeseed oil
4 small white mushrooms, finely sliced
1 Cox's apple, cored, peeled and coarsely grated
2 walnut halves, roughly crushed, to garnish

PREPARATION TIME: 5 minutes

1 Mix the lemon juice, mustard, salt, pepper, sugar, if using, and oil in a small basin, then toss in the apples and mushrooms.

2 Serve in a pretty bowl sprinkled with the walnuts.

SHIRRED EGGS WITH PRAWNS AND TOMATOES

SERVES 1

10 g (¼ oz) butter
1 medium tomato, skinned, seeded and diced
25 g (1 oz) shelled prawns, fresh or frozen
salt
freshly ground black pepper
2 eggs (size 1)
1 tablespoon cream
tip of a knife-point ground coriander (optional)
1 teaspoon freshly snipped herbs, e.g. chives, parsley, marjoram, basil

PREPARATION TIME: 10 minutes
COOKING TIME: about 10 minutes

1 You will need 2 small non-stick pans for this dish. In the first melt the butter and add the diced tomato, then the prawns and just heat through: don't overcook. Season lightly with salt and pepper.

2 Beat the eggs with the cream and pour into the second pan. Season with salt, pepper and coriander, if using.

3 Using a straight-edged wooden spatula, over a minimal heat, draw the eggs across the bottom of the pan each time they start to set. When just cooked but still somewhat creamy, spoon on to a warm serving plate.

4 Using a slotted spoon, spoon over the tomato and prawns. Sprinkle with the herbs and serve at once.

Sunday Brunch

CREAMED EGGS WITH FRESH HERBS

HOME-MADE SAUSAGES

A GOOD BLOODY MARY

SPECIAL SUNDAY KEDGEREE

RAGOÛT OF VEAL KIDNEYS

*B*runch or late breakfast is an ideal way of passing a couple of hours with friends. Here are some main courses ideal for such an occasion.

Whether you offer a cheering glass is optional: a good breakfast coffee and an astringent tea, preferably a single blend such as Darjeeling or Yunnan.

Have everything ready before your guests arrive, leaving just a few minutes to finish things off. Have rolls or croissants on an oven tray ready to warm through and if you are serving toast, then cut and crust the bread and cover with a cloth at the ready for the toaster.

The luxury of a honeycomb is a nice notion and certainly your own home-made jam or marmalade can be used effectively.

Kidneys in some form or another are such a part of the Great British Breakfast that they have to be included somewhere. However, you either love 'em or hate 'em, so offer an attractive alternative, which could be simply scrambled eggs with fresh herbs, kedgeree or grilled home-made sausages.

If you choose not to serve alcohol then a glass of Fresh fruit juice over cracked ice (page 30) would make an exceedingly good apéritif.

CREAMED EGGS WITH FRESH HERBS

SERVES 4

8 eggs (size 1)
4 tablespoons double cream
salt
freshly ground white or black pepper
15 g ($\frac{1}{2}$ oz) butter
1 heaped tablespoon snipped fresh chives
1 heaped tablespoon finely chopped fresh parsley
1 level tablespoon of one of the following: basil, tarragon, golden marjoram

PREPARATION TIME: 12–15 minutes
COOKING TIME: 3–4 minutes

You will need a 1$\frac{3}{4}$ litre (3 pint) non-stick pan.

1 Beat the eggs, add the cream and season lightly with salt and pepper.

2 Melt the butter in a 1.75 litre (3 pint) non-stick pan without browning. Pour in the egg and cream mixture and, using a straight-edged wooden spatula over a low heat, draw the eggs across the bottom of the pan each time they start to set. Whilst they are still creamy but not fully set, sprinkle over and mix in the herbs.

3 Spoon into a warm serving dish and serve as soon as possible as the eggs quickly harden and, whilst totally edible, are not quite as nice as they are when still creamy.

HOME-MADE SAUSAGES

SERVES 4

1 egg (size 1)
1 teaspoon salt
1 teaspoon ground ginger
1 teaspoon ground mace
1 × 175 g (6 oz) skinned and boned chicken breast, diced
1 × 175 g (6 oz) rasher of green gammon, diced
175 g (6 oz) lean pork, diced
50 g (2 oz) pork fat, diced
1 small Cox's apple, not peeled, coarsely grated
flour to dredge
soy oil and a knob of butter (optional) for frying

PREPARATION TIME: 30 minutes
COOKING TIME: 8–10 minutes

1 Run a food processor fitted with the steel blade or use a regular mincing machine. (The texture will be different depending which you use: smooth with the processor and coarser with the mincer.) Put in the egg and seasonings and gradually add all the meats and the apple.

2 Scrape on to a floured board and divide into 12 even-sized balls. Dipping the hands into cold water between each process, form and roll the minced mixture into sausage shapes approximately 7.5 cm (3 inches) long. A

3 Roll each sausage in flour and arrange on a plate. Chill until ready to fry.

4 Heat 3 mm ($\frac{1}{8}$ inch) soy oil in a large 30 cm (12 inch) frying pan. Add the knob of butter, if used, swirling this around to ensure even melting. When smoking lightly, and using 2 palette knives or 2 spoons, arrange the sausages in the pan. Seal over a good heat on all sides. Lower the heat and continue frying turning at half-minute intervals until just cooked through.

5 Drain on crumpled paper towels. Serve on a warm dish.

A The sausages can be prepared to this stage and refrigerated overnight, covered with cling film.

Home-made sausages; Creamed eggs with fresh herbs; A good bloody Mary

A GOOD BLOODY MARY

MAKES 6–8 GLASSES

1 × 1 litre (1$\frac{3}{4}$ pint) jar of good quality tomato juice
juice of $\frac{1}{2}$ large lemon
1 tablespoon Worcestershire sauce
2 dashes Tabasco sauce
1 teaspoon celery salt
1 glass of Amontillado sherry
vodka (preferably Wyborova)
celery sticks, to garnish

PREPARATION TIME: 5 minutes

It is said that only men can mix good drinks. I know differently, as this recipe from a friend demonstrates.

1 Make up the tomato juice mixture (leaving out the vodka) in a glass jug the evening before your party.

2 On the day, fill a large glass with ice cubes. Pour over a double vodka. Fill up with the tomato juice mixture and add a stick of celery for guests to stir things themselves.

SPECIAL SUNDAY KEDGEREE

SERVES 4

4 eggs
175 g (6 oz) long-grain rice
salt
50 g (2 oz) butter
1 small onion, finely sliced
100 g (4 oz) button mushrooms, finely sliced
2 tablespoons flour
tip of a teaspoon curry powder
½ chicken or vegetable stock cube
600 ml (1 pint) milk
1 × 225 g (8 oz) tin middle-cut salmon (or 350 g (12 oz)
piece cooked fresh salmon or smoked haddock)
freshly ground black pepper
juice of ½ lemon
150 ml (¼ pint) single cream (optional)
fresh parsley

PREPARATION TIME: 15 minutes, plus cooling
COOKING TIME: 35 minutes

*T*he word Kedgeree stems directly from the Hindi word *khichri* – and belongs to what I call the 'Raj' dishes; those dishes much beloved adapted from the Indian cuisine to suit the Colonels and their ladies.

I doubt that any self-respecting Indian would recognize the versions made in this country, least of all mine, but it's *so* good for late breakfast or brunch it's not to be missed!

I sometimes serve the rice separately, as it is possible to make it look more attractive this way, particularly if you mould the rice in a buttered ring-mould first, then fill the centre with the salmon (or haddock), eggs and mushrooms in their creamy sauce. The ring-mould will take double the quantity of rice.

1 Boil the eggs for not more than 10 minutes from cold (they should still have a 5 mm (¼ inch) of soft centre). Run them under cold water until they are quite cold, then shell them. Cut them into quarters, then into eighths. Cover with foil until required.

2 Cook the rice in plenty of boiling lightly-salted water for 17 minutes exactly, then run it under the cold tap to wash off the starch. Leave to drain in a sieve or colander.

3 Melt the butter in a pan which will be large enough to contain all the ingredients. Add the sliced onions and fry until golden brown, then add the mushrooms and fry for a few seconds before stirring in the flour.

4 Add the touch of curry powder and crumble in the piece of stock cube. Gradually work in the cold milk a little at a time until you have a smooth sauce and simmer for 5 minutes, stirring to ensure that it doesn't stick or burn.

5 If using tinned salmon, pour the juices from the tin into the sauce. Taste and adjust the seasoning, adding pepper if necessary and add lemon juice to acidulate lightly. Skin and flake the fish and fold into the sauce, then fold in the cooked rice and gently allow this to heat through, stirring with a 'folding' action as you do so, so that you do not break up the fish too much.

6 Finally, just before you are ready to serve the kedgeree, carefully fold in the eggs. If the finished dish is too solid for you, bring the cream to the boil in a small pan, then add to the kedgeree. Spoon into a heated dish, sprinkle with parsley and serve.

Special Sunday Kedgeree; Ragoût of veal kidneys

RAGOÛT OF VEAL KIDNEYS

SERVES 4–6

3 calves' or 12 lambs' kidneys
100 g (4 oz) buttom mushrooms
50 g (2 oz) butter
¼ teaspoon powdered rosemary or ginger
salt
freshly ground black pepper
2 tablespoons Madeira or medium dry sherry
150 ml (¼ pint) double cream

PREPARATION TIME: 20 minutes
COOKING TIME: about 10 minutes

1 Skin and trim kidneys of all fat, then either cut them in half or slice them thinly. Wipe and coarsely slice the mushrooms.

2 Melt the butter in a frying pan until it foams and fry the kidneys until they are tender, 3–4 minutes. If your pan is not very large, it is better to do this in 2 batches. Season the kidneys lightly with rosemary or ginger, salt and pepper and remove them to a warm serving dish.

3 Toss the mushrooms in the remaining pan juices, adding a little more butter if necessary. Pour over the Madeira or sherry and the cream, then cook until the sauce has a good creamy consistency. Pour over the kidneys and serve straight away.

My Special Treat-Yourself Breakfast

OGEN MELON WITH ORANGE

PARMA HAM WITH LEMON JUICE

The breakfasts on pages 26–31 are ideal for almost any occasion except for those, perhaps all too rare, occasions when you want to give yourself a treat.

Here is my personal scheme for this occasion. What I most enjoy is quite simple to prepare, but it never fails to please me and here's what it is. I follow the melon and Parma ham with wholemeal toast spread with acacia honey and I quench my thirst with China tea and a little milk.

OGEN MELON WITH ORANGE

SERVES 1

1 small ripe Ogen melon
1 naval orange
1 good squeeze lemon juice
1 teaspoon sugar

PREPARATION TIME: 5 minutes, plus chilling overnight

This also makes a good starter for a dinner party, when a tablespoon of Cointreau can be added to each melon.

1 Cut a lid out of the melon about 2.5 cm (1 inch) down, holding the point of the knife at 45° downwards angle. Slice a sliver off the base, so that the melon stands firm. Using a teaspoon, scoop out the seeds.

2 Finely grate ½ teaspoon of the zest of the orange, then segment the orange flesh. Fill the melon with the orange segments.

3 Mix the lemon juice, sugar and zest together and pour over the orange pieces.

4 Replace the melon lid. Cover with cling film and chill, preferably overnight, until ready for use.

5 Serve on a plate or fruit saucer, with a dessertspoon and fork.

PARMA HAM WITH LEMON JUICE

SERVES 1

75-100 g (3–4 oz) Parma ham (Prosciutto) or cured
Westphalia or York ham
½ lemon wrapped in a piece of clean muslin
pepper mill filled with black pepper
wholemeal toast, to serve

PREPARATION TIME: 2 minutes

1 Arrange the ham in swathes on a dinner plate with the lemon wedge. Place the pepper mill alongside. Serve together with a basket of brown wholemeal toast thickly cut and a pot of chilled, unsalted butter.

Ogen melon with orange; Parma ham with lemon juice

Weekend Breakfast for Four

FRESH FRUIT JUICE OVER CRACKED LEMON ICE

CROISSANTS OR BRIOCHES

*W*ith guests to stay for the weekend, the importance of breakfast will rest less in the food than in the creation of a relaxed 'Sunday' atmosphere, when the tensions of the working week can be well and truly dispersed. It is mostly prepared beforehand and so can be ready at whatever time your guests feel like rising.

There will be other times during the weekend when you can go to town over the food, so in my book the breakfast is a simple 'continental' affair. But, a treat there has to be, and in this case it comes in the form of the freshly squeezed orange juice – a deliciously refreshing drink and a great way to start the day.

This is the one time when a knife and fork and a flower posy can be an impediment as you attempt to leaf through the papers. A basket of warm croissants or brioches, a couple of slices of moist, crisp wholemeal toast, plenty of unsalted butter and a pot well filled with Black Cherry Jam are all that is needed for this leisurely session.

FRESH FRUIT JUICE OVER CRACKED LEMON ICE

SERVES 4

4 lemons
juice of 4 large sweet oranges
800 ml (1⅓ pints) apple juice
4 sprigs mint or orange slices to garnish

PREPARATION TIME: 5 minutes, plus freezing

Any left-over cubes are good with gin and tonic!

1 Fill 2 ice-cube trays almost to the top with water. Pour into a measuring jug.

2 Squeeze the lemons. Strain into the jug of water. Pour back into the ice-cube tray and freeze.

3 Turn out 8–10 lemon ice cubes per glass on to a clean cloth. Cover and crush with a rolling pin.

4 Put the cracked ice into 4 tall 350 ml (12 fl oz) glasses and pour over the strained orange juice. Fill up with apple juice and tuck in a sprig of mint or an orange slice to garnish.

CROISSANTS

MAKES 6

450 ml ($\frac{3}{4}$ pint) milk
15 g ($\frac{1}{2}$ oz) fresh yeast, crumbled or 3.5 g ($\frac{1}{8}$ oz) easy-blend dried yeast
500 g (1 lb 2 oz) fine plain white flour, sieved
15 g ($\frac{1}{2}$ oz) salt
100 g (4 oz) butter
beaten egg for glazing

PREPARATION TIME: 40 minutes, plus proving and resting overnight
COOKING TIME: about 25 minutes
OVEN: 220°C, 425°F, Gas Mark 7

Recipes for these crescent-shaped buns vary in richness, from very flaky, pastry-type affairs to a more bread-like consistency. I prefer the latter. There was a time in 18th-Century England when we actually had something like the croissant: they were called 'wigs'. My recipe is similar.

1 Warm 125 ml (4 fl oz) of the milk to blood heat (about 38°C, 98.4°F) and pour into a bowl. Mix in the yeast and work to a soft dough with 100 g (4 oz) of the flour. Leave to develop and rise to double its size in a lightly greased bowl covered with a cloth. This will take up to an hour.

2 When risen, add the rest of the milk and dredge in the remaining flour and salt. Mix together, then turn on to a lightly floured surface and knead with the heel of the hand, pushing away from you. You don't have to be quite so forceful as with bread, just knead until you have a firm but flexible dough.

3 Roll the dough into an oblong roughly 35 × 40 cm (14 × 16 inches) and 1 cm ($\frac{1}{2}$ inch) thick.

4 Spread the butter over the whole surface area of the rolled dough. Fold top to middle and bottom over top, then turn, so that the edges are in the same position as a closed book. Press all the edges together with the rolling pin. Leave in the refrigerator for an hour.

5 Roll again in a similar fashion, leaving the dough to rest for an hour after this. Repeat again; this time leaving overnight in the refrigerator in a plastic bag lightly dredged with flour.

6 Roll out the pastry to a rectangle approximately 30 cm (12 inches) long, 10–13 cm (4–5 inches) wide and 5 mm ($\frac{1}{4}$ inch) thick. Cut into 10–13 cm (4–5 inches) squares. Cut these diagonally into 2 triangles. Roll up loosely from the long edge to the point. Seal the point with a little beaten egg. Form into crescent shapes, nipping and sealing the edges together with a little beaten egg. Leave to rise again until doubled in size.

7 Now pull the joined tips slightly apart, brush with beaten egg and bake in a preheated oven for approximately 20–25 minutes.

BRIOCHES

MAKES ABOUT 12–16

225 g (8 oz) plain white flour, sieved
15 g ($\frac{1}{2}$ oz) fresh yeast or 3.5 g ($\frac{1}{8}$ oz) easy-blend dried yeast
1 teaspoon salt
15 g ($\frac{1}{2}$ oz) caster sugar
2–3 tablespoons milk
2 eggs (size 1), beaten
75 g (3 oz) unsalted butter, softened to a paste
extra beaten egg for glazing

PREPARATION TIME: 50 minutes, plus proving
COOKING TIME: 15 minutes
OVEN: 220°C, 425°F, Gas Mark 7

Francophiles adore these yeast-like cakes, with their appealing fluted sides. Some say that brioches have their origins in Brie – hence the name – but this might well be disputed by the Swiss and Austrians who appear to have adopted them as their national bread.

They take a bit of effort and time, and the little ones are certainly more reliable to make than large ones, but they're both well worth the effort. They freeze well, so if you do embark on making them, make a lot and freeze them in appropriate batches.

1 Put 50 g (2 oz) of the flour into a bowl. Make a well and crumble in the yeast very finely. Add 2 tablespoons warm water and, using the fingertips, work into a smooth paste. Form this into a ball.

2 Take a small pan or bowl of lukewarm water, drop the ball of dough into it and leave to develop and rise in volume, about 8–10 minutes.

3 Meanwhile, mix the salt and sugar with the remaining flour. Add the milk and eggs. It is quite a messy business to work this into a dough, but you must do so. When you have a workable mass, which doesn't stick to the fingers, add the butter and work this into the dough. Don't try adding any extra flour, just persevere.

4 Remove the risen yeast dough from the water and, using the fingers, spread out like a fan. Let it drain for a minute or so on a clean towel. Now knead lightly but thoroughly with the second paste. Put into a floured plastic bag and leave to rise and develop for 3–4 hours in a warm part of the kitchen (not on top of the central heating).

5 Next knock the dough down, but not as laboriously as you would do for bread. Place on a floured tray, cover

with a clean, floured cloth and leave in a *cold* place or refrigerator to firm up and take on a manageable consistency, about 45 minutes.

6 Knead lightly and form into egg-sized balls. Cut off one-third of each ball and form into smaller balls with little points at one end.

7 Lightly butter your brioche tins. Put in the larger of the 2 balls. Make a small incision and fit in the pointed end of the smaller of the balls. (This is to give them their mini cottage loaf shape when baked.)

8 Leave to prove again for 15 minutes in a warmer place than previously – the top of the boiler is good.

Brioches; Croissants

9 Brush the top of each brioche with a little beaten egg. Bake in a preheated oven for 15 minutes. Turn out on to a wire tray to cool. F Serve with morning coffee or creamy hot chocolate.

F Freeze for up to 6 weeks. Thaw overnight at room temperature, then refresh in a hot oven for 10 minutes.

Lunch

'I just have an apple and a piece of cheese for lunch.'
How often do we hear that said in this rat-race of a world,
and what a pity it is that the days of the long leisurely
lunch seem to have disappeared. But this need not be
so, for lunchtime, particularly at weekends, is an ideal
time to enjoy entertaining your friends or family.
Think of the plus factors. It's daylight, and, in the Spring
and Summer seasons, England is at its glorious best.
Lunch is usually a less expensive meal to provide,
being composed of lighter, more casual dishes.
Dressing, too, can be more relaxed and people enjoy a
midday drive out to see friends.
Certainly lunch-time entertaining — like brunch or
breakfast and involving only a little more effort - is
becoming more popular. Here are some ideas for you to
consider when you next have guests at midday.

Lunch with a Friend

FRITTATA

FRISÉE SALAD WITH HONEY

GRAPES WITH BLUE CHEESE FILLING

This is the sort of lunch you would serve when the friend is in the 'best mate' category and is just as likely to be a parent, sister, brother, aunt, uncle or godmother. Food should be tasty but not elaborate and, as with all entertaining, you won't want to be in the kitchen for more than the few minutes it will take to cook the Frittata and toss the salad.

Everyday table linen and place mats can be used but add the extra touch of warm rolls or garlic bread nestling in a basket between colourful, starched wraps. Enjoy a leisurely bottle of wine and serve coffee in cups or mugs if you wish. Sit back and have a really good chat.

FRITTATA

SERVES 2

2 tablespoons olive or soy oil
1 small onion, finely sliced or chopped
2 small boiled new potatoes, diced
$\frac{1}{2}$ small red pepper, thinly sliced
6 black olives, pitted and quartered
50 g (2 oz) grated Gouda or full fat soft cheese
1 tablespoon snipped chives or chopped parsley, or both!
8 thin slices dried sausage, such as pepperoni or salami or 2 big rashers bacon, fried crisp
1 tomato, quartered
6 eggs, beaten and seasoned with a little salt, pinch of mace and freshly ground black pepper

PREPARATION TIME: 20 minutes
COOKING TIME: 19–20 minutes
OVEN: 200°C, 400°F, Gas Mark 6

This frittata is a delicious oven-baked omelette.

1 Pour the oil into a 20–23 cm (8–9 inch) seamless non-stick Victoria sponge tin. Add the onion and bake in the preheated oven for about 7–8 minutes until *almost* soft. (Crispness is desirable but not always liked!)

2 Arrange all the other ingredients apart from the eggs ad lib over the onions, then pour over the seasoned beaten egg mixture.

3 Return to the oven and bake for 10–12 minutes, when the frittata will be puffed up. It should not however be

4 Serve cut in wedges with Frisée Salad.

Frittata with Frisée salad with honey; Grapes with blue cheese filling

FRISÉE SALAD WITH HONEY

SERVES 2

8–10 nice frisée (curly endive) leaves, or use Iceberg or Boston lettuce, well washed, torn into pieces and patted dry

DRESSING
25 ml (1 fl oz) olive or soy oil
strained juice of ¼ lemon
1 teaspoon mild flower honey
½ teaspoon mild French mustard
salt
freshly ground black pepper

PREPARATION TIME: 10 minutes

1 Arrange the salad leaves in a bowl. Put all the dressing ingredients in a screw-top jar and shake to mix well.

2 Sprinkle the dressing over the leaves, then toss until well coated.

3 Arrange nicely on 2 salad plates.

GRAPES WITH BLUE CHEESE FILLING

SERVES 2

75 g (3 oz) blue cheese
squeeze of lemon juice
2 dashes Tabasco sauce
6 large black grapes, halved and seeded
6 large green grapes, halved and seeded
15 g (½ oz) nib almonds or desiccated coconut

PREPARATION TIME: 20 minutes

1 Rub the blue cheese through a sieve on to a small plate. Mash with a fork whilst adding the lemon juice and Tabasco sauce.

2 Sandwich each grape together with a teaspoon of the soft cheese mixture. Dip the open edge in the nuts or coconut, then chill. Ⓐ

3 Serve on a dish covered with a doily. These filled grapes can be eaten with the fingers.

Ⓐ These can be prepared the day before and kept chilled.

Special Lunch for Two

TARTLET OF QUAILS' EGGS WITH COTTAGE CHEESE AND SMOKED SALMON

BUTTER ROAST POUSSIN WITH PÂTÉ AND MADEIRA CREAM SAUCE

GLAZED CARROT STICKS WITH GINGER AND ORANGE

STRAWBERRIES WITH PORT AND RASPBERRY SAUCE

Lunch time is the ideal time to entertain a special friend. It can be seen as an opportunity to enjoy some of those luxuries, those things you might normally by-pass when cooking for larger numbers. I'm talking of those gastronomic luxuries, such as fresh lobster mayonnaise, a small pot of foie gras, oysters or Scotch smoked salmon cut wafer-thin: the main dish could be a succulent butter roast poussin with an elegant side salad of one of the latest discoveries – corn salad, fresh dandelion tips, trevise, or radicchio – followed by delicious strawberries perfumed with port as the light, simply prepared dessert.

Such an occasion is the time when the convenience of luxury foods can be used to great effect; a time-liberator if you like.

Consider a change in your usual pattern of dining: arrange a smaller table to the side of the room, rather than use only one end of your normal dining table. Position the 2 chairs, at adjacent points of the compass for intimacy or opposite, ideal for earnest talk. This is an opportunity to use your prettiest table linen and to bring out any individual serving dishes you are particularly fond of. It is almost more important to make sure that those thoughtful little extras are provided: a posy of exotic flower heads and the hand-made chocolates, for example.

Ask your guest to come at 1 o'clock and have the tartlets in the dining room ready to serve, so that you can sit down with your friend and plunge straight into a good chat.

TARTLET OF QUAILS' EGGS WITH COTTAGE CHEESE AND SMOKED SALMON

SERVES 2

PASTRY CASES:
100 g (4 oz) butter and lard mixed
175 g (6 oz) plain flour
50 g (2 oz) Parmesan cheese, freshly grated
salt
cayenne pepper
1 egg yolk

FILLING:
50 g (2 oz) cottage cheese
squeeze of lemon juice
salt
freshly ground black pepper
50 g (2 oz) smoked salmon, diced
4 quails' eggs, hard-boiled for 3 minutes, shelled and cut into halves

GARNISH:
4 pieces smoked salmon, rolled
snipped chives and paprika or a few juicy capers
25 g (1 oz) caviar or lumpfish roe

PREPARATION TIME: 30 minutes, plus chilling
COOKING TIME: 15–20 minutes
OVEN: 190°C, 375°F, Gas Mark 5

It is uneconomical to make pastry for 2, so make this quantity, which will yield 10–12 tartlets, and freeze the remainder or make pastry biscuits for cocktail time.

1 To make the pastry cases, rub the fats into the flour. Toss in the cheese, ½ teaspoon salt and a pinch of cayenne pepper. Mix the egg yolk with 2 tablespoons cold water, add to the flour and bind the mixture into a dough. Leave for 30 minutes.

2 Butter 2 × 7.5 cm (3 inch) shallow, shaped tartlet tins and place on a baking tray. Roll out the dough to line the tins.

3 Bake in a preheated oven for 15–20 minutes until the pastry is crisp and pale brown. Cool a little. Remove from the tins and place right side up on a cooling tray.

4 To make the filling, mix the cottage cheese with the lemon juice, salt and pepper. Mix in the smoked salmon, then chill well.

5 Put into the baked pastry shells just before serving. Sit 4 quails' egg halves on top of each tartlet. Garnish with a roll of smoked salmon and a sprinkling of snipped chives and paprika or with capers, or real salmon caviar.

BUTTER ROAST POUSSIN WITH PÂTÉ AND MADEIRA CREAM SAUCE

SERVES 2

100 g (4 oz) butter, softened
½ garlic clove, crushed
pinch of ground mace
salt
freshly ground black pepper
2 × 225–350 g (8–10 oz) poussins
2 rashers of streaky bacon
2 small slivers of onion
¼ teaspoon flour
½ teaspoon tomato purée
¼ chicken stock cube
120 ml (4 fl oz) dry Madeira
150 ml (¼ pint) single cream
2 butter-fried croûtons
1 × 50 g (2 oz) tin pâté de foie gras or Swiss parfait

PREPARATION TIME: 20 minutes
COOKING TIME: 45–50 minutes
OVEN: 240°C, 475°F, Gas Mark 9
then: 200°C, 425°F, Gas Mark 7

1 Blend the butter, garlic, mace, ½ teaspoon salt and a few twists of pepper into a paste. Rub this all over and inside each bird, then cover each breast with a rasher of bacon.

2 Sit each bird on a sliver of onion in a small roasting tin. Roast the birds near the top of a preheated oven. After 15 minutes lower the heat and continue roasting for a further 15–20 minutes according to how pink you like your game.

3 Remove the birds with the onion and keep warm. Drain off the excess fats from the juices in the roasting tray, then pour the remaining juices into a pan. Sprinkle in the flour and add the tomato purée. Brown the mixture very gently over a low heat.

4 Crumble the piece of stock cube into the juices, add the Madeira and bring to the boil. Reduce the heat and simmer for 2 minutes, then add the cream. Simmer for a further minute or so.

5 To serve, strain the sauce into a warm boat. Spread the butter-fried croûtons with pâté and arrange on the plate with the poussins.

GLAZED CARROT STICKS WITH GINGER AND ORANGE

SERVES 2

8 new carrots or 4 small-to-medium older ones
300 ml (½ pint) orange juice
¾ chicken stock cube
1 teaspoon ground ginger
¼ teaspoon salt
½ garlic clove, uncrushed
25 g (1 oz) unsalted butter

PREPARATION TIME: 10 minutes
COOKING TIME: 10 minutes

1 Peel and trim the carrots. Cut lengthways into 1 cm (½ inch) thick slices, then into 5 mm (¼ inch) thick sticks. Put the orange juice into a saucepan with the stock cube, ginger and salt and bring to the boil.

2 Cook the carrots in the orange mixture for 3–4 minutes, so they are still slightly crisp. Drain, retaining the liquid. Add the garlic to the liquid and reduce by boiling rapidly until thickened.

3 Remove the garlic from the pan, add the butter and cooked carrot sticks and toss them over the heat until completely coated with the glaze and heated through.

Butter roast poussin with pâté and Madeira cream; Glazed carrot sticks with ginger and orange; Strawberries with port and raspberry sauce

STRAWBERRIES WITH PORT AND RASPBERRY SAUCE

SERVES 2

175 g (6 oz) strawberries
120 ml (4 fl oz) ruby port
100 g (4 oz) frozen raspberries
juice of ½ lemon
25 g (1 oz) caster sugar
merest pinch ground mace

PREPARATION TIME: 10 minutes, plus chilling
COOKING TIME: about 1 minute

1 Hull and quarter the strawberries. Bring all the remaining ingredients to the boil. Lower the heat and simmer for 15–20 seconds, then rub through a fine sieve.

2 Sprinkle the surface of the sauce with a little caster sugar to prevent a skin forming and allow to cool.

3 In a bowl carefully fold the quartered strawberries into the sauce to coat their cut surfaces. Chill well covered with cling film. Ⓐ

4 Serve, piled up in a bowl.

Ⓐ This sweet can be made the day before and kept chilled.

An Easy Picnic on the Beach for Four

CHILLED PEA AND HAM SOUP

SESAME SEED ROLLS

BOOKMAKER'S SANDWICH WITH REMOULADE RELISH

RASPBERRY COCONUT SLICE

I think – if I'm being truly honest – that my beach is somewhere in the Mediterranean or Florida and not one of those surrounding our shores.

My menus are for the grown-ups, for they are the ones who need entertaining. Children, on the other hand, like food which does not detract from their beach games or exploration: Scotch eggs (with the option of an added spoonful of sandwich spread), home-made sausage rolls, spicy chicken drumsticks, simple well-filled sandwiches, cheese shortbreads, sticks of celery, filled on the spot with cream cheese, a Thermos jug filled with cubes of chilled fruit plus the inevitable chocolate bar are all that are needed for the minors' end of the family.

For us, a flask of well-chilled soup of a drinkable consistency is as simple a starter as you will find. Sips from a cup of a delicious pea and ham soup will raise the odd eyebrow, and the Bookmaker's sandwich is easy to cope with and does not require a cluster of implements, nor do the other things I would take to the beach.

A large cool box is, however, essential, as those of you who travel to foreign parts will well know, for butter can cause havoc when temperatures soar above the seventies.

CHILLED PEA AND HAM SOUP

SERVES 4–6

1 × 750 g (1½ lb) ham or bacon knuckle
2.25 litres (4 pints) cold water
300 ml (½ pint) dry white wine (German type)
1 sprig thyme
1 small bay leaf
2 teaspoons white peppercorns
1 carrot, peeled and roughly chopped
1 leek, split and washed
1 onion, peeled and quartered
2 stalks celery, roughly cut up
350 g (12 oz) frozen petits pois
salt, if necessary

PREPARATION TIME: 20–25 minutes, plus cooling overnight
COOKING TIME: about 4 hours

1 Put the knuckle in a pan of cold water. Bring to the boil and discard the water.

SESAME SEED ROLLS

*T*hese can be served hot or cold, and go well with all the soups. Allow 2 slices of white bread per serving. Remove the crusts and roll the slices flat with a heavy rolling pin.

Butter each rolled slice liberally, sprinkle with a level teaspoon of sesame seeds, a modest pinch of salt and a sprinkling of freshly ground black pepper. Roll them up from corner to corner with the seeds on the outside and bake them in an oven preheated to 200°C, 400°F, Gas Mark 6, until they are golden brown and crisp right through, about 30 minutes. You may have to turn them a time or two to ensure this.

You can vary the flavour of these rolls by spreading them with different savoury butters. Serve hot or cold.

BOOKMAKER'S SANDWICH WITH REMOULADE RELISH

SERVES 4

a little olive oil
12 thin slivers of fillet steak 5 mm ($\frac{1}{4}$ inch) thick
salt
freshly ground black pepper
1 French stick split and spread with butter or mayonnaise and French mustard
8 sprigs watercress

PREPARATION TIME: 5 minutes
COOKING TIME: 5–8 minutes

This sandwich is said to be popular with the Irish racing fraternity!

1 Heat the oil in a heavy frying pan until smoking. Add the steak, sear and seal quickly on both sides. Season well with salt and pepper and cook to your liking – ideally, charred and rare, so that the juices soak into the bread.

2 Arrange the steaks along half the split bread. Cover with watercress. Put the other half of the bread on top and press for 15 minutes under a weighted kitchen board. Cut into 1 cm ($\frac{1}{3}$ inch) thick diagonal slices.

3 Serve with Remoulade relish (made by mixing 2 tablespoons strained Piccalilli with 150 ml ($\frac{1}{4}$ pint) mayonnaise and adding a little piccalilli juice if necessary) and a tossed salad.

2 Refill the pan with the 2.25 litres (4 pints) of water. Add all the remaining ingredients except the peas and salt. Bring to the boil slowly, then reduce the heat and simmer for 4 hours.

3 Strain through a fine mesh strainer, retaining the knuckle and leave to cool. Strip only the lean meat from the knuckle and mince or shred.

4 Skim the surface fats off the cooled liquid and discard. Measure 1.2 litres (2 pints) of this stock into a pan containing the peas. (You could reserve a few peas for garnish if serving this at home.) Bring to the boil, simmer for 5–6 minutes, then strain into a bowl.

5 Put the cooked peas in a blender or food processor and purée. Mix back into the pea stock. Check the seasoning – the knuckle may be salty enough for your palate. Cool, then chill overnight.

6 Serve in chilled soup cups with a little of the shredded bacon. Add a few of the reserved peas as an attractive garnish, if using.

Above: Chilled pea and ham soup; Bookmaker's sandwich with remoulade relish; Sesame seed rolls

RASPBERRY COCONUT SLICE

MAKES 16–20 SQUARES

100 g (4 oz) lard
25 g (1 oz) butter
200 g (7 oz) plain flour
175 g (6 oz) unsalted butter
175 g (6 oz) caster sugar
finely grated rind of 1 lemon
3 eggs (size 1), lightly beaten
1 tablespoon self-raising flour
275 g (10 oz) desiccated coconut
350 g (12 oz) raspberry jam

PREPARATION TIME: 30 minutes
COOKING TIME: 35–40 minutes
OVEN: 190°C, 375°F, Gas Mark 5

The children will want to share these tasty treats.

1 Mix the lard and butter into the flour in a bowl until the mixture resembles breadcrumbs. Add enough water to mix to a smooth dough, then roll out to line a 35 × 23 cm (14 × 9 inch) Swiss roll tin. You should have enough pastry left over to make a lattice top.

2 Cream the unsalted butter and sugar with the finely grated lemon rind. Beat in the eggs slowly, then fold in the flour. Finally, mix in the desiccated coconut.

3 Spread the jam evenly over the bottom of the pastry-lined tin. Spoon over the coconut mixture, spreading evenly. Re-roll the pastry trimmings and cut into strips 1 cm (½ inch) wide. Arrange the strips in a lattice pattern over the top of the coconut. Place the tin on a preheated baking sheet and bake in a preheated oven for 35–40 minutes, until lightly golden. Leave to cool.

4 Cut into squares or fingers and store in an airtight tin in layers separated by greaseproof paper.

Summer Lunch for Four in the Garden

WATERCRESS MOUSSE

SALADE NIÇOISE WITH HOT GRILLED FRESH TUNA FISH

RHUBARB ICE CREAM WITH GIN

My attitude to serving lunch al fresco is to transfer out-of-doors that scheme of things (china, cutlery, napkins, etc), which you would have arranged indoors. Admittedly I do not dine outside often, due more to the irritation of the insects than to the inclemency of the weather. When I do, I like to provide comfortable chairs with arms, supplemented by cushions, shade and a rafia fan for each guest to deal with the flies and wasps. Similarly I like dress to be crisp and elegant rather than over-casual.

It does seem appropriate to have cold food but with just one hot item to give an extra dimension. The tuna fish is grilled indoors to retain the element of surprise: the cold dishes can wait in the refrigerator or freezer. Put the wine at the ready outside in a cooler somewhere discreet and you can also prepare the coffee in advance and serve it from one of the newer, smart Thermos jugs.

WATERCRESS MOUSSE

SERVES 6–8

225 g (8 oz) full fat soft cheese
150 ml (¼ pint) mayonnaise
1 sachet gelatine crystals
150 ml (¼ pint) hot light chicken stock
4 bunches watercress, washed and trimmed
a few dashes Tabasco sauce
salt
freshly ground black pepper
150 ml (¼ pint) double or whipping cream
endive and radish, to garnish

PREPARATION TIME: 20 minutes, plus chilling

1 Beat the cheese until smooth, then mix in the mayonnaise. Sprinkle the gelatine on to the hot stock and cool.

2 Place the watercress, including the small stalks, and the cooled gelatine liquid in a food processor or liquidizer and purée. Add the Tabasco and salt and pepper.

3 Whip the cream until it *just* holds soft peaks. Cut and mix into this the mayonnaise and cheese mixture, then cut and mix in the watercress purée. Pour into 6–8 individual ramekins, or into a 900 ml (1½ pint) dish or mould. Chill. Garnish before serving.

SALADE NIÇOISE WITH HOT GRILLED FRESH TUNA FISH

SERVES 4

4 × 2.5 cm (1 inch) thick, centre-cut fresh tuna steaks, each about 100 g (4 oz)

MARINADE:
2 tablespoons olive oil
1 tablespoon red wine vinegar
1 shallot, finely chopped
1 garlic clove, crushed
freshly ground black pepper

SALAD:
3 medium-to-hard-boiled eggs, quartered
6–8 lettuce leaves
2 tomatoes, sliced
10–12 slices of peeled, seeded cucumber
4 rings of green pepper, seeded
8 chicory leaves
8 sprigs of watercress
1 small onion, peeled and sliced

DRESSING:
3 tablespoons olive or soya oil
1¼ tablespoons red wine vinegar
1 teaspoon French mustard
small clove of garlic (optional), finely chopped

GARNISH:
8 black or green olives
8 anchovy fillets
1 tablespoon capers

PREPARATION TIME: 40 minutes, plus marinating overnight
COOKING TIME: 4 minutes

If fresh tuna is not available, use halibut or turbot pieces.

1 Cut each piece of fish equator-wise into 2 pieces. Mix the marinade ingredients together, then pour over the fish, cover and leave overnight.

2 Assemble the salad on 4 plates. Put all the dressing ingredients into a screw-topped jar and shake until well mixed. Taste and adjust the seasoning.

3 Remove the fish from the marinade and sear under a hot grill or in a heavy-bottomed frying pan, lightly oiled. Baste with the marinade and cook for 2 minutes only on each side. Arrange the hot pieces on top of the salad. Garnish with olives, anchovies and capers.

RHUBARB ICE CREAM WITH GIN

SERVES 4–6

1 kg (2 lb) rhubarb, trimmed and cut into 2.5 cm (1 inch) pieces
25 ml (1 fl oz) gin
15 g (½ oz) unsalted butter
100 g (4 oz) caster sugar
1 tablespoon cold water

SYRUP:
175 g (6 oz) caster sugar
2 tablespoons cold water

PREPARATION TIME: 15 minutes, plus freezing
COOKING TIME: about 25 minutes

1 Put the rhubarb, gin, butter, sugar and water into a pan. Cover and toss over a low heat until the juices start to draw, then simmer until the rhubarb has pulped. Pour into a liquidizer or food processor and blend, then rub through a fine sieve. Do not cool yet.

2 To make the syrup, bring the sugar and water to the boil and continue boiling until the 'hard ball' stage, 125°C/256°F. If you don't possess a sugar thermometer, boil rapidly until the sugar is making a 'rich' bubbling noise, is thick and *just about* to turn colour: you will notice this beginning to happen if you watch the edges of the syrup as it boils. Do not stir. Mix this syrup into the rhubarb purée.

3 Now cool and churn in the ice-cream maker for 20 minutes to a soft, spoonable texture. It will look pale-pink and creamy. If you do not have a churn pour the cooled mixture into a freezer container and freeze. Beat twice at hourly intervals using a balloon whisk. Freeze until ready for use. F

F Freeze for up to 3 months.

Salad niçoise with hot grilled fresh tuna fish; Rhubarb ice cream with gin

Sunday Lunch for Six on a Cold Day

PARCELS OF HAM AND CHICKEN MOUSSELINE
WITH LEMON SAUCE

OLD ENGLISH DUCK PIE WITH FORCEMEAT
BALLS AND CHESTNUTS

SOFT CHEESE-STUFFED POTATOES

BROCCOLI, CAULIFLOWER AND ORANGE SALAD

CARAMEL CREAM WITH CARAMEL BAKED PEARS

Those marvellous cold days, with their silvery light, frost-etched trees and huge orange sun low in the sky, call for a richly-filled savoury pie as the centre of attraction at lunch time. After a brisk walk, muffled up to your ear tips and with snow crunching underfoot, it is the type of day to bring a glow to the cheeks and a feeling of well-being to all.

Just to watch the crisp, golden crust being cut and the abundant filling being spooned out will instantly warm your guests. Top and tail the main course with what you will, this traditional dish will be the centre of attraction, as it sits in its deep dish, with crinkly-edged and splendidly decorated pastry and the tip of a novel pie funnel peering through the centre of the crust. Add chunks of wholemeal bread, pots of butter, wedges of Stilton and dices of mature Cheddar to the menu and a friendly fire in the hearth and you will have a splendid menu to keep the cold well at bay.

PARCELS OF HAM AND CHICKEN MOUSSELINE WITH LEMON SAUCE

SERVES 6

175 g (6 oz) raw lean gammon
175 g (6 oz) raw chicken breast
$\frac{1}{4}$ teaspoon ground nutmeg
1 teaspoon salt
1 teaspoon finely grated lemon rind
$\frac{1}{2}$ teaspoon freshly ground white pepper
or $\frac{1}{4}$ teaspoon ground ginger
2 eggs, beaten
150 ml ($\frac{1}{4}$ pint) double cream
24 Chinese cabbage leaves
chicken stock, made from a carcass or a stock cube
(see method)

SAUCE:
2 egg yolks (size 1)
$\frac{1}{4}$ teaspoon salt
juice of 1 lemon
1 tablespoon water
100 g (4 oz) butter, melted and kept hot
50 ml (2 fl oz) double cream, warmed
6 spring onions, washed and finely shredded

PREPARATION TIME: 45 minutes, plus chilling overnight
COOKING TIME: 20–25 minutes

1 Place the ham and chicken meat in a liquidizer or food processor, together with the nutmeg, salt, lemon rind and pepper or ginger, and process to a purée. Mix in the eggs, scrape the mixture into a bowl and beat in the cream. Chill well (overnight or all day).

2 Wash the Chinese leaves. Bring a pan of lightly salted water to the boil and blanch the leaves, a few at a time, for 30 seconds. Rinse under cold water and pat with paper towels to dry.

3 Clear a work surface. Arrange 2 leaves in a cross and put a spoonful of the purée in the centre. Wrap the stalk ends over first, then the green ends over the top to make a neat parcel.

4 Tie with fine string or linen thread. Place the parcels in a shallow pan, barely cover them with stock and poach for 12–15 minutes, until the filling has firmed up.

5 Meanwhile, make the sauce. Mix the egg yolks, salt, lemon juice and water in a heatproof glass bowl. Stand the bowl over a pan of hot water and whisk gently until the mixture thickens. Remove the bowl from the heat.

6 Dribble in the hot melted butter, whisking hard and allowing the emulsion to thicken as you do this. Stir in the cream. Add the raw spring onion before serving. Do not reheat the sauce.

7 Remove the string from the meat parcels and serve 2 per person. If necessary, these will keep warm in the oven at 140°C, 275°F, Gas Mark 1 for about 20 minutes. In which case, place the parcels on a warm dish and cover with a clean napkin which has been dipped in scalding water and wrung out.

Parcels of ham and chicken mousseline with lemon sauce

OLD ENGLISH DUCK PIE WITH FORCEMEAT BALLS AND CHESTNUTS

SERVES 6

FORCEMEAT BALLS:
175 g (6 oz) lean pork or veal, cut up
100 g (4 oz) pork fat, cut up
1 teaspoon ground nutmeg
2 tablespoons medium sherry
1 egg, beaten
2 teaspoons salt
1 duck liver, diced
oil for frying

FOR THE PIE:
1 × 1.75 kg (4 lb) duck, cut up and liver reserved
1 teaspoon flour
225 g (8 oz) bacon, cut into sticks
1 onion, chopped
225 g (8 oz) oyster or field mushrooms, quartered
rind and juice of 1 orange
½ bottle red wine
½ × 300 ml (½ pint) can duck or game consommé
salt
freshly ground black pepper
1 sprig fresh or 1 teaspoon dried sage
1 sprig fresh or 1 teaspoon dried thyme
1 garlic clove, crushed
1 × 225 g (8 oz) can chestnuts in brine rinsed, or fresh roasted chestnuts, skinned
1 × 350 g (12 oz) packet flaky pastry, or 350 g (12 oz) total weight home-made shortcrust pastry (page 16)

PREPARATION TIME: 45 minutes
COOKING TIME: about 2 hours
OVEN: 200°C, 400°F, Gas Mark 6; then: 230°C, 450°F, Gas Mark 8; finally: 180°C, 350°F, Gas Mark 4

Have your poulterer cut the duck into first 4, then 8 pieces, removing excess carcass bones, which can be used for stock for soup. The pie is equally good served cold with a crisp green salad.

1 To make the forcemeat balls, put the pork or veal and fat twice through the fine blade of a mincer or place in a liquidizer or food processor and purée. Mix in the nutmeg, sherry, beaten egg and salt, adding the duck liver last to retain texture.

2 Form into 12–14 small flattish balls or cakes. Heat a little oil in a frying pan until smoking, then brown the forcemeat quickly and set aside.

3 Brown the duck pieces a few at a time in the oil, then transfer to an ovenproof dish. Sprinkle over the flour and mix in well.

4 In the pan juices, brown the bacon sticks, onion and mushrooms. Remove with a draining spoon and transfer to the ovenproof dish. Add the orange rind and juice, wine and enough consommé just to cover. Sprinkle over the salt, pepper, herbs and garlic. Cover and cook in a preheated oven for 45 minutes.

5 Remove the duck pieces to a deep pie dish, about 25 × 18 × 10 cm (10 × 7 × 4 inches). For those who don't like the rich duck skin, remove at this point.

6 Disperse the chestnuts and forcemeat balls among the duck pieces. Skim the excess fat from the sauce and pour over the contents of the pie dish. (This sauce is quite thin.) Leave it to cool.

7 Roll out the pastry, cut a strip and fit round the rim of the pie dish. Cut and fit a lid; decorate with leaves.

8 Brush the pie all over with beaten egg, raise the oven temperature and bake for 15 minutes, then reduce the temperature and cook for a further 45 minutes.

SOFT CHEESE-STUFFED POTATOES

SERVES 6

3 medium potatoes
oil, butter or bacon fat for coating
175 g (6 oz) full fat soft cheese
25 g (1 oz) butter, softened
half a bunch of spring onions, chopped
salt
freshly ground black pepper

PREPARATION TIME: 10 minutes
COOKING TIME: about 1 hour 10 minutes
OVEN: 200°C, 400°F, Gas Mark 6

1 Rub the potato skins with oil, butter or bacon fat to make them crisp, then bake in a preheated oven for about 1 hour.

2 Cream the cheese and butter together. Cut the potatoes in half, scoop out the flesh and mash well. (Do not use a food processor as this will make it glutinous!)

3 Beat in the cheese mixture and half the spring onions. Season well with salt and pepper, then pile back into the empty shells. Ⓐ

4 Return to the oven to heat through. Sprinkle with the remaining onions and serve piping hot.

Ⓐ Can be prepared to this point the day before.

BROCCOLI, CAULIFLOWER AND ORANGE SALAD

SERVES 6

DRESSING:
85 ml (3 fl oz) olive or soy oil
juice of ½ orange
1 teaspoon grated orange zest
1 tablespoon red wine vinegar
1½ teaspoons mild French mustard
1 teaspoon caster sugar
1 garlic clove, crushed
tip of a knife ground mace or nutmeg
salt
freshly ground black pepper

SALAD:
2 whole oranges
1 small cauliflower, trimmed
equal proportion of good firm broccoli spears

PREPARATION TIME: 30 minutes, plus draining
COOKING TIME: 3–4 minutes

1 Place all the ingredients for the dressing in a screw-top jar and shake until well mixed. Store, refrigerated.

2 Using a sharp knife, peel and segment the oranges into a bowl, reserving the skins. Cut the cauliflower and broccoli into even-sized pieces, leaving on plenty of stalk but cutting through this and the flower, lengthways.

3 Bring a large pan of salted water to the boil, together with the orange skins. Toss in the vegetables and cook for 3–4 minutes only, leaving them still quite crisp.

4 Drain, discard the orange skins and cool under running cold water to retain their bright white and green colour. Leave to drain for 30 minutes.

5 Arrange attractively with the orange segments on a glass platter or in a salad bowl. Cover with cling film and chill. A Just before serving, spoon over the dressing.

A Can be prepared the day before, covered with cling film and kept chilled.

Old English duck pie; Cream cheese-stuffed potatoes; Broccoli, cauliflower and orange salad

CARAMEL BAKED PEARS

SERVES 4

4 ripe pears
juice of 1 lemon
225 g (8 oz) caster sugar
300 ml ($\frac{1}{2}$ pint) double cream (optional)

PREPARATION TIME: 10 minutes, plus chilling
COOKING TIME: about 2$\frac{1}{4}$ hours
OVEN: 160°C, 325°F, Gas Mark 3

Warning! Do not touch hot caramel at *any* stage with your bare hands.

1 Peel, core and cut each pear in half. Toss the pieces in the lemon juice.

2 Bring the sugar and 300 ml ($\frac{1}{2}$ pint) water to the boil in an aluminium or stainless steel pan, or a copper sugar boiler. Boil without stirring to a dark caramel colour.

3 Arrange the pears in 1 layer in a shallow ovenproof dish. Pour over the caramel.

4 Bake, uncovered, in a preheated oven for 2 hours or until the pears are nicely caramelized and the sauce dark and viscous – but don't let it get too hard.

5 Place the pears in a serving dish with some of the caramel, but reserve at least 150 ml ($\frac{1}{4}$ pint) for the sauce. Leave to chill.

6 To make the caramel whipped cream sauce, if serving, whip the cream to soft peak, then stir in the remaining caramel. Serve the sauce separately.

CARAMEL CREAM

SERVES 4–6

CARAMEL:
75 g (3 oz) caster sugar
$\frac{1}{4}$ teaspoon cream of tartar

CUSTARD:
50 g (2 oz) caster sugar
5 eggs, plus 1 extra yolk
300 ml ($\frac{1}{2}$ pint) milk
300 ml ($\frac{1}{2}$ pint) single cream
vanilla pod or $\frac{1}{2}$ teaspoon vanilla essence

PREPARATION TIME: 20 minutes, plus chilling
COOKING TIME: 1–1$\frac{1}{4}$ hours
OVEN: 160°C, 325°F, Gas Mark 3

1 First make the caramel to coat a 900 ml (1$\frac{1}{2}$ pint) mould. Put the sugar in a pan with a little water and the cream of tartar. Bring to the boil, stirring until the sugar is evenly dissolved. Don't stir again, or crystals will form. Reduce the heat and leave the sugar to caramelize slowly until dark brown.

2 Have ready a sink of cold water to plunge the bottom of the pan in as soon as you think it is ready. Pour the caramel into the mould and swirl round until the mould is completely coated. You will need oven gloves or cloths for this, as it is hot work!

3 Now make the custard: have a bain-marie of hot water ready. Cream the sugar and eggs and egg yolk together until pale and thickened. Place the milk, cream and vanilla together in a saucepan and bring slowly to the boil.

4 Pour this over the egg mixture, stirring well, then strain the custard into the caramel-lined mould.

5 Place in the bain-marie and cook for 45 minutes–1 hour, or until the custard is set. Cool, then chill.

6 To unmould, run a hot, wet palette knife round the sides of the mould and insert on to a shallow dish.

A Glamorous Fork Lunch for Twelve

CHILLED TOMATO, STRAWBERRY AND RHUBARB
SOUP

CHICKEN WITH GINGER IN MADEIRA CREAM
SAUCE

RICE PILAF WITH MUSHROOMS, BACON AND
CELERY

CUCUMBER, ORANGE AND COCONUT SALAD

ROSE PETAL BAVAROIS MERINGUE

PEACHES IN BRANDY

*T*here are occasions when a fairly formal affair is required, yet there is not enough space to seat everyone comfortably. It is on just such an occasion that the fork lunch comes into its own.

The idea comes from America, the menu offered should be strictly fork food, namely dishes presented in such a way that they can be eaten with style and grace using just a fork (or spoon for the soup or dessert).

General guidance on the types of food to serve, presentation and organization are given in the introduction (page 6).

CHILLED TOMATO, STRAWBERRY AND RHUBARB SOUP

SERVES 12

1 kg (2 lb) ripe red tomatoes, halved, seeded
750 g (1½ lb) strawberries, hulled, and cut in half
1 kg (2 lb) pink rhubarb, trimmed, cut up
1.75 litres (3 pints) rich chicken stock, page 22
2 teaspoons salt
3–4 teaspoons freshly ground white pepper
300 ml (½ pint) double cream (optional), to serve

GARNISH:
225 g (8 oz) strawberries, hulled, sliced and lightly peppered
2 tablespoons freshly snipped chives

PREPARATION TIME: 30 minutes, plus chilling overnight
COOKING TIME: 10–15 minutes

The secret of this soup if secret there be is the rich chicken stock and the essential condiment of freshly milled white pepper, which marries with the strawberries in a magical way. Stock cubes may be used but the strawberry flavour will be dimmed.

1 Put the tomatoes, strawberries and rhubarb into a 4.5 litre (8 pint) stainless steel or enamel pan (aluminium will make the soup lose its colour) and cover with the cold stock. Add the salt and pepper. Bring to the boil and simmer until the fruits are soft, about 10 minutes.

2 Pour through a fine-meshed wire sieve into a bowl. Rub and scrape the pulp through until you are left with no more than a tablespoonful of debris. This is arduous but necessary! Cool, then chill.

3 Serve in chilled bowls with a swirl of cream if using and 3–4 slivers of strawberry on the top together with a sprinkling of chives.

FAR LEFT: Caramel cream; Caramel baked pear. LEFT: Chilled tomato, strawberry and rhubarb soup

CHICKEN WITH GINGER IN MADEIRA CREAM SAUCE

SERVES 12

25 ml (1 fl oz) soy or olive oil
225 g (8 oz) blanched whole almonds
2 × 1½ kg (3½ lb) fresh chickens, jointed or 8 chicken breasts,
boned
2 tablespoons olive oil
50 g (2 oz) butter
salt
freshly ground black pepper
1¼ teaspoons ground ginger
2 garlic cloves, crushed
2 × 2½ cm (1 inch) pieces green ginger, very finely sliced
120 ml (4 fl oz) dry Madeira or Amontillado sherry
300 ml (½ pint) double cream
2 tablespoons snipped chives or flat-leafed parsley, to garnish

PREPARATION TIME: 45 minutes
COOKING TIME: 20 minutes

1 Heat the soy or olive oil in a large frying pan. Add the almonds, lower the heat and fry until evenly golden brown, stirring continuously as almonds readily burn. Salt them lightly and drain in a metal sieve. Ⓐ

2 Using kitchen scissors, clip off all skin and fat and any wayward pieces of bone or sinew from the chicken. Next cut the flesh into 4 cm (1½ inch) sections, then cut each section into even, bite-size pieces approximately 5 mm (¼ inch) thick. Ⓐ

3 Mix all the meat together and divide into roughly 4 batches. Heat a third of the oil and butter in a large frying pan until hot and giving off an almond aroma.

4 Working with a straight-edged wooden spatula, fry the first batch of chicken quickly (about 1 minute) over a good heat. Season towards the end with salt, pepper and some of the ground ginger. Scatter in some garlic and green ginger and pour in a little of the Madeira or sherry, then let it sizzle and bubble for half a minute more. Transfer to a flameproof casserole. Repeat this process until you have fried all the chicken. Ⓐ

5 Pour over the cream, bring to the boil and bubble for 2–3 minutes, until the sauce is smooth and nicely coats each bit of chicken. Stir in the almonds. Transfer to a warm serving dish and scatter over the chopped herbs.

Ⓐ The almonds can be prepared several days in advance and stored in a plastic bag in the refrigerator.
The chopped chicken flesh can be prepared the day before, covered and kept chilled.
The chicken can be cooked to this stage 1–2 days in advance, covered and kept chilled.

RICE PILAF WITH MUSHROOMS, BACON AND CELERY

SERVES 12

350 g (12 oz) long-grain rice
50 g (2 oz) butter or soy oil
100 g (4 oz) unsmoked long back bacon, diced and rinded
100 g (4 oz) onion, very finely chopped
1 small head celery, washed and cut into 3 mm (⅛ inch) dice
1 large garlic clove, crushed
salt
225 g (8 oz) tiny button mushrooms, wiped and quartered
approx. 1 litre (35 fl oz) boiling chicken stock or 1 chicken
stock cube and 1 litre (35 fl oz) boiling water

GARNISH:
100 g (4 oz) unsalted butter (optional)
50 g (2 oz) freshly ground Parmesan cheese

PREPARATION TIME: 30 minutes
COOKING TIME: 30–35 minutes
OVEN: 220°C, 425°F, Gas Mark 7

1 Put the rice in a measuring jug and note its volume. Melt the butter or soy oil in a large, 4.5 litre (8 pint) flame and ovenproof pan until foaming. Add the bacon and onion and fry over a good heat until golden brown.

2 Next add the celery and fry for 1 minute, then put in the rice and continue frying, stirring well with a straight-edged spatula, for another minute or so.

3 Add the garlic, and (depending on how salty the stock is) season with salt, then stir in the mushrooms. Ⓐ

4 Bring the stock to a rolling boil. Measure exactly 2½ times the volume of the rice and pour over the rice and vegetable mixture. Bring everything back to the boil, stirring continuously.

5 Cover and transfer the pan to the preheated oven for exactly 20 minutes. When you take the lid off, there should be a cushion of mushrooms across the top and it will be obvious that the stock has been absorbed. If not turn off the heat and leave the pan in the oven for an extra 3–4 minutes. If the dish has to be kept waiting, keep it warm at 110°C, 225°F, Gas Mark ¼.

6 Just before serving, using a dinner fork, stir in the butter (if used) and grated Parmesan cheese. Spoon the mixture into double moulds, pack in well, then turn out on to the serving plates. Alternatively, transfer to a serving dish. The taste will not suffer if kept warm after adding the butter and cheese, but the pilaf will go somewhat 'sticky'.

Ⓐ Can be prepared to this stage 1–2 days in advance, covered and kept chilled.

CUCUMBER, ORANGE AND COCONUT SALAD

SERVES 12

DRESSING:
finely shredded zest of 1 orange
juice of $\frac{1}{2}$ an orange
juice of $\frac{1}{2}$ a lemon
2 teaspoons mild French mustard
25 ml (1 fl oz) rich olive or nut oil
salt
freshly ground black pepper
1 teaspoon caster sugar
1 small clove garlic, crushed
2 tablespoons fresh oregano when available

SALAD:
3 large cucumbers
4 navel oranges, segmented
2 tablespoons desiccated coconut

PREPARATION TIME: 20 minutes

1 Place all the ingredients for the dressing in a screw-topped jar and shake well together.

2 Using a swivel blade peeler, peel the cucumbers, then cut the flesh in half lengthways. Scoop out the seeds with a teaspoon or melon baller and discard. Cut on the diagonal into 3 mm ($\frac{1}{8}$ inch) pieces.

3 Put the cucumber, orange segments and dressing in a large bowl. Toss everything together scattering the coconut in as you do so. Transfer the salad to a clean bowl to serve.

Cucumber, orange and coconut salad; Rice pilaf with mushrooms, bacon and celery; Chicken with ginger in Madeira cream sauce

ROSE PETAL BAVAROIS MERINGUE

SERVES 8–10

4 eggs, separated
225 g (8 oz) caster sugar
15 g ($\frac{1}{2}$ oz) powdered gelatine
4 tablespoons triple strength rosewater
300 ml ($\frac{1}{2}$ pint) creamy milk
almond oil for greasing
300 ml ($\frac{1}{2}$ pint) double or whipping cream
sugar-frosted rose petals, to decorate
extra cream, to decorate

PREPARATION TIME: 1 hour, plus chilling overnight
COOKING TIME: 1$\frac{1}{2}$ hours
OVEN: 110°C, 225°F, Gas Mark $\frac{1}{4}$

A light creamy centre with an intriguing flavour reminiscent of Turkish Delight is surrounded by crisp meringue fingers. Serve with a raspberry or redcurrant purée made by gently cooking the fruit with sugar to taste until the skins are soft. Purée, sieve, then sharpen with a little lemon juice if liked.
The meringue fingers can be purchased to save time.

1 Using 2 egg whites and 100 g (4 oz) of the sugar make up a meringue mixture in the usual way. Spoon into a piping bag fitted with a plain 1 cm ($\frac{1}{2}$ inch) fluted nozzle.

2 Line a baking sheet with non-stick silicone paper and pipe fingers of meringue approximately 6 cm (2$\frac{1}{2}$ inches) long – you will need about 20. Cook in a preheated oven until crisp, about 1$\frac{1}{2}$ hours. Leave them to cool.

3 Sprinkle the gelatine over the rose-water in a small bowl. Heat the milk in a non-stick pan, then whisk together the 4 egg yolks and remaining sugar until thick and creamy.

4 Whisk in the hot milk, pour back into the pan and heat very gently, stirring constantly with a straight-edged wooden spatula until the mixture coats the back of the spatula leaving a distinct, clean trail when the finger is drawn across.

5 Remove from the heat and whisk in the gelatine mixture until dissolved. Cool the custard until beginning to set.

6 Lightly oil the sides and bottom of a 1.2 litre (2 pint) straight-sided soufflé dish and line with a circle of non-stick paper at the bottom.

7 Whisk the remaining egg whites to stiff peaks and whip the cream to soft peak. Cut and fold first the cream, then the egg whites into the custard.

8 Spoon evenly into the prepared soufflé dish. Cover with cling film and chill overnight or until set.

9 To serve, unmould the bavarois on to a flat serving dish. Arrange the meringue fingers on end around the sides of the bavarois gently pressing into place, securing them with a blob of extra whipped cream if necessary. Take some pale pink rose petals, brush with egg white and dust with caster sugar. Arrange on top of the bavarois.

PEACHES IN BRANDY

SERVES 6–8

8 ripe peaches
75 g (3 oz) caster sugar
juice of 1 lemon
50 ml (2 fl oz) brandy (or whisky)

PREPARATION TIME: 20 minutes, plus marinating overnight

1 Plunge the peaches 2 at a time into a pan of boiling water for 20 seconds. Remove with a draining spoon to a bowl of ice-cold water, then peel off the skins.

2 Cut the peaches in half and take out the stone. Cut into crescents, put into a non-metal bowl, then sprinkle with the sugar, lemon juice and brandy. Cover with cling film and chill overnight.

LEFT: Rose petal bavarois meringue; Peaches in brandy

A Vegetarian Buffet for Sixteen to Twenty

POMPIAN SOUP

GNOCCHI ALLA ROMANA WITH FRESH TOMATO
SAUCE

BAKED COURGETTES WITH PEPPERS,
MOZZARELLA CHEESE AND ALMONDS

NEW CAULIFLOWER CHEESE

TABBOULEH EGGS

SAVOURY WALNUT ROULADE WITH ASPARAGUS
TIPS

GREEN BEAN AND MUSHROOM SALAD

SWEET CUCUMBER SALAD WITH FRESH DILL

SLICED TOMATOES WITH GINGER

*A*s someone who enjoys an evil treat once in a while, I
have included in my vegetarian buffet menu one or
two truly rich dishes – the creamy multi-toned soup and
the roulade. However, a little should go a long way when
included alongside the other dishes.

I have suggested soup as a starter for the simple reason
that it is of a totally different texture from the main dishes
and can be served hot or chilled depending on whether
your party is a summer or winter affair.

The courses will give slightly more than a tasting of each
for 16 people and if you serve the menu as it stands then
there is ample for up to 20 guests. Serve wholemeal or herb
breads if you wish, and try spreading them with cream
cheese or mayonnaise instead of butter for a change. Finish
off with a simple, purchased water ice.

POMPIAN SOUP

SERVES 16–20

50 g (2 oz) butter or olive oil
225 g (8 oz) onion, skinned and chopped
2 small garlic cloves, crushed
*750 g (1¼ lb) pumpkin (or melon), weighed after peeling and
seeding*
*350 g (12 oz) freshly boiled and skinned chestnuts, or
chestnuts in brine, strained*
2 vegetable stock cubes, crumbled
4 × 5 cm (2 inch) slivers of orange rind
1 teaspoon ground ginger
2 teaspoons sweet mild paprika
1 teaspoon freshly ground white or black pepper
1 teaspoon salt (or to taste)
2 sachets saffron powder (optional)
1.2 litres (2 pints) fresh orange juice
600 ml (1 pint) cold water
300 ml (½ pint) single cream

GARNISH:
fine strips of orange zest, blanched

PREPARATION TIME: 30 minutes
COOKING TIME: 20 minutes, plus reheating

This rich warm-toned soup where all the autumn flavours
are combined can be served hot or chilled. It is very rich, so
serve in small (teacup) quantities. Pompian was an 18th
century word for a pumpkin.

1 Melt the butter or oil and fry the onion over a low heat
until transparent but not coloured.

2 Add the garlic and pumpkin or melon. Cook gently
until the juices 'draw', stirring from time to time.

3 Add all the remaining ingredients apart from the cream
or chicken stock and simmer, covered, until the
pumpkin or melon is tender. Pass through a mouli or
blender, then rub through a fine sieve. Cool, then chill.

4 To serve chilled, chill the cream and stir into the soup.
To serve hot, bring the soup to boiling point, stir in the
cream, then bring back to just under boiling.

5 Garnish each serving with slivers of orange rind. Peeled
and skinned orange segments may be served as an
accompaniment, if liked.

GNOCCHI ALLA ROMANA WITH FRESH TOMATO SAUCE

SERVES 16–20

1¼ litres (2½ pints) rich milk
1¼ teaspoons salt
300 g (11 oz) semolina
150 g (5 oz) freshly grated Parmesan
120 g (4½ oz) butter
3 egg yolks
¾ teaspoon grated nutmeg

TOMATO SAUCE:

750 g (1½ lb) tomatoes, skinned, seeded and chopped
1½ dessertspoons dry sherry
250 ml (8 fl oz) tomato juice
1½ teaspoons caster sugar
1 large sprig dill or mint
3 teaspoons lemon juice
salt
freshly ground white pepper

PREPARATION TIME: 30 minutes, plus cooling
COOKING TIME: 45–55 minutes
OVEN: 230°C, 450°F, Gas Mark 8

1 Bring the milk and salt to the boil, then lower the heat. Sprinkle in the semolina, stirring and beating all the time with a balloon whisk. Cook this mixture over a low heat for 15 minutes, when it will be very thick.

2 Add half the grated cheese, 25 g (1 oz) of the butter and the egg yolks, beating each in well as you work. Dampen a work surface and tip the mixture out on to it. Wet your right hand and press the mixture into a squarish shape, about 1 cm (½ inch) thick (less if anything), then leave to cool completely (about 1½ hours).

3 Using a plain scone cutter or drinking glass 5 cm (2 inches) in diameter cut the mixture into discs, dipping the cutter into cold water between each cut.

4 Butter an ovenproof dish. Cut the leftovers of the gnocchi mixture into 2.5 cm (1 inch) bits and lay them in the bottom of the dish. Dot with some of the remaining butter and dredge with a little cheese.

5 Arrange the discs, overlapping slightly, on top of this, dot each disc with the remaining butter and scatter over the rest of the cheese and the nutmeg. Bake in a preheated oven for 15–20 minutes or until a golden brown crust has formed.

6 Meanwhile, make the tomato sauce. Put all the ingredients into an enamel pan and simmer until reduced to a fine pulp.

7 Press the sauce through a fine sieve, reheat and serve with the gnocchi.

Gnocchi alla Romana with fresh tomato sauce; Pompian soup

BAKED COURGETTES WITH PEPPERS, MOZZARELLA CHEESE AND ALMONDS

SERVES 8–16

1 each red, yellow, green peppers (or 3 red)
3 tablespoons olive oil
1 onion, chopped
2 garlic cloves, crushed
8 × 10 cm (4 inch) long courgettes, topped and tailed
salt
freshly ground black pepper
lemon juice
50 g (2 oz) whole blanched almonds (optional)
175 g (6 oz) Mozzarella cheese or cottage cheese

PREPARATION TIME: 45 minutes
COOKING TIME: about 1 hour
OVEN: 240°C, 475°F, Gas Mark 9 (to roast peppers); then:
200°C, 400°F, Gas Mark 6

This dish can be served as an accompaniment to roast meats, or chilled and used as a first course. If you choose to do the latter, substitute cottage cheese, as Mozzarella toughens when cold.

1 Roast the peppers in the preheated oven until the skins blister – they may well char a little, but this doesn't matter. Leave to cool a little, then peel, seed and chop into 3 mm ($\frac{1}{4}$ inch) dice.

2 Heat the oil, add the onion and cook over a low heat until soft but not brown. Add the chopped peppers and garlic and cook gently for 10 minutes.

3 Meanwhile, bring a large pan of salted water to the boil and cook the courgettes for 7–8 minutes. Drain and, when cool enough to handle, cut them in half. Scoop out 1 cm ($\frac{1}{2}$ inch) of the flesh, using a melon baller or teaspoon. Chop this flesh, add it to the peppers and cook the mixture for a further 2–3 minutes.

4 Arrange the courgettes in a buttered baking dish. Season them with salt, pepper and a good squeeze of lemon juice. Put 2–3 almonds (if using) in each shell. Fill with the pepper mixture. Top with pieces of Mozzarella or cottage cheese. Bake at the lower temperature for 30 minutes, until browned, hot and bubbling.

NEW CAULIFLOWER CHEESE

SERVES 16–20

2 heaped tablespoons freshly grated Parmesan cheese
1 garlic clove, crushed
$\frac{1}{2}$ teaspoon ground mace
300 ml ($\frac{1}{2}$ pint) single cream
juice of $\frac{1}{2}$ lemon, strained
2 medium white cauliflowers broken into 2.5 cm (1 inch) long florets
salt if necessary
chopped fresh parsley, to garnish

PREPARATION TIME: 30 minutes, plus standing
COOKING TIME: 5–8 minutes

I tackled the task of restyling this dish to fit the mood and taste of the 1980s by referring back, as I very often do, to the methods of the 1700s. I think that this is one of my great discoveries.

1 The secret of success with this dish is to mix the cheese, garlic, mace and cream together in a saucepan and allow to stand for 2 hours.

2 Bring some salted water to the boil, add the lemon juice, then drop in the cauliflower florets and cook for 2–3 minutes. The cauliflower should remain crisp. Drain well. A

3 Add the cauliflower to the pan containing the cream mixture and toss and bubble over a medium to high heat until each floret is well coated, and all is well blended. Taste and add salt if necessary. Serve garnished with chopped fresh parsley.

A The cauliflower can be cooked in advance, rinsed under cold running water to cool completely, then drained well. Reheat with the cream mixture over a low heat, tossing and stirring well until piping hot.

TABBOULEH EGGS

Tabbouleh eggs; Baked courgettes with peppers, mozzarella cheese and almonds; New cauliflower cheese

SERVES 8–16

225 g (8 oz) bulgar wheat (cracked wheat)
vegetable stock, to cover
200 ml ($\frac{1}{3}$ pint) olive oil
2 teaspoons mild French mustard
juice of 1 large lemon
3 large tomatoes, skinned, seeded, diced
2 bunches spring onions, trimmed with as much of the green left on as possible, then chopped
1 heaped teacup freshly chopped parsley
1 heaped teacup freshly chopped mint
salt
freshly ground black pepper
sprig of fresh mint, to garnish

TO SERVE:
8 hard-boiled eggs
about 85 ml (3 fl oz) French dressing

PREPARATION TIME: 45 minutes, plus soaking

1 Place the wheat in a large bowl and cover with the cold stock, leave for 1 hour during which time it will swell. Drain and squeeze out surplus moisture, then spread the soaked wheat on a clean tea towel to dry a little.

2 Mix the oil, mustard and lemon juice together in a large bowl, then mix in all the rest of the tabbouleh ingredients. Cover and chill until ready for use.

3 To serve, shell and cut the hard-boiled eggs in half. Splash well with a little French dressing (about 1 teaspoon on each) and arrange over the tabbouleh. Garnish with a sprig of fresh mint.

SAVOURY WALNUT ROULADE WITH ASPARAGUS TIPS

SERVES 8–16

4 large eggs
salt
freshly ground black pepper
225 g (8 oz) walnuts, crushed

SAUCE:
½ vegetable stock cube
3 tablespoons red wine vinegar
juice of ½ an orange
4 egg yolks
175 g (6 oz) hot melted butter
peel of 1 large orange, pared, finely chopped, blanched and drained
mace

FILLING AND GARNISH:
1 bundle fresh young asparagus, lightly cooked, tips only
4 hard-boiled eggs, quartered or 12 quails' eggs, boiled, shelled and halved
2 tablespoons snipped chives
50 g (2 oz) pistachio nuts, shelled and roughly chopped (optional)

PREPARATION TIME: 30 minutes
COOKING TIME: about 15 minutes
OVEN: 200°C, 400°F, Gas Mark 6

1 Butter and line a Swiss roll tin with buttered paper.

2 Whisk the eggs with the salt and pepper until thick, fold in 100 g (4 oz) of the crushed walnuts and pour into the prepared tin, spreading the mixture evenly into the corners. Bake near the top of the oven for 6–8 minutes until firm to the touch in the centre.

3 Put a clean tea towel, wrung out in cold water, on to a flat surface. Cover with a piece of greaseproof paper spread evenly with the remaining crushed walnuts. Invert the roulade on to the walnuts and remove the base paper to allow the steam to escape. Then roll loosely. [A]

4 To make the sauce, crumble the stock cube into the vinegar and orange juice in a saucepan and boil until reduced to 2 tablespoons. Whisk the egg yolks and the reduced liquid in a bowl over gently boiling water until thick but not curdled. Remove from the heat and beat in the melted butter, drop by drop at first, then in a steady stream, whisking briskly all the time. Add the orange peel and season with salt, pepper and mace. [A]

5 Set aside 2 tablespoons of the sauce, 6 asparagus tips and 5 or 6 egg quarters (or quails' eggs halves) for decoration.

6 Unroll the roulade, spread with some of the sauce and arrange the asparagus tips, eggs and chives on top. Re-roll the roulade and decorate by spooning the remaining sauce along the centre, arranging asparagus tips and quails' egg halves on the sauce, and sprinkling with roughly chopped pistachio nuts if used.

[A] The roulade can also be served cold. Leave it loosely rolled until you wish to fill it. The sauce can be made in advance and kept in the refrigerator overnight, where it will thicken slightly.

CLOCKWISE FROM THE TOP: Sweet cucumber salad with fresh dill; Green bean and mushroom salad; Sliced tomatoes with ginger; Savoury walnut roulade with asparagus tips

1. Bruschetta - Tomato/onion salsa ✓
   & salad   Red Pepper antipasta ✓
   (cheese + cuc.   Mushroom marinated.

2. Salmon - Potatoes, stuffed courgettes
               Green veg. , cucumber top. (marinate

3. Meringue "nest" - cream/rasp. + choc.

Need = white wine vinegar for marinade
       bread for brushetta.

GREEN BEAN AND MUSHROOM SALAD

SERVES 16–20

1 kg (2 lb) young green beans, trimmed

DRESSING:
300 ml ($\frac{1}{2}$ pint) olive oil
65 ml ($2\frac{1}{2}$ fl oz) sherry or red wine vinegar
2 tablespoons mild French mustard
$\frac{1}{4}$ teaspoon grated nutmeg
salt
freshly ground black pepper
350 g (12 oz) white button mushrooms, finely sliced

GARNISH:
1 tablespoon snipped fresh chives
2 tablespoons chopped fresh parsley
2 tablespoons crushed salted peanuts

PREPARATION TIME: 30 minutes, plus chilling
COOKING TIME: 2–3 minutes

1 Blanch the beans in salted boiling water for 2–3 minutes. Cool under running cold water. Drain well and chill.

2 Put the oil, vinegar, mustard, nutmeg, salt and pepper in a large screw-top jar and shake until blended.

3 Put the beans and mushrooms in a large bowl, pour over the dressing and mix well. Pile into a large serving dish and sprinkle with the chives, parsley and peanuts.

SWEET CUCUMBER SALAD WITH FRESH DILL

2 cucumbers, sliced paper-thin
salt

DRESSING:
150 ml ($\frac{1}{4}$ pint) olive or soy oil
65 ml ($2\frac{1}{2}$ fl oz) lemon juice
3 teaspoons caster sugar
1 garlic clove, crushed
1 teaspoon mild French mustard
$\frac{1}{4}$ teaspoon white pepper
2 tablespoons finely snipped fresh dill weed or mint

PREPARATION TIME: 10 minutes, plus draining

1 Put the cucumber into a colander, sprinkling *lightly* with salt as you go along.

2 Put a plate and a heavy weight on top to press out the juices. Leave for an hour or so, then squeeze out excess juice with a clean hand and transfer to a large bowl.

3 Put all the dressing ingredients in a screw-top jar and shake together until creamy and the sugar is dissolved. Mix this with the squeezed cucumber. Transfer to a clean serving dish and scatter with the dill or mint.

SLICED TOMATOES WITH GINGER

6 large firm tomatoes
salt
freshly ground black pepper
ground ginger
3 pieces stem ginger, chopped
1 tablespoon freshly chopped oregano

1 Skin and slice the tomatoes, then lay in layers in a shallow serving dish. Dredge each layer with a little salt, pepper and ground ginger.

2 Sprinkle over the stem ginger and oregano.

Tea

*Afternoon Tea is the one meal unique to the British
tradition. We, or rather Anne, Duchess of Bedford,
invented it some 200 years ago. The nibbles taken secretly
by Her Grace in the confines of her boudoir to assuage the
hunger pangs she felt during what was for her the
interminable wait between luncheon and dinner quickly
caught on with the leisured classes and grew in popularity
right up to World War II.*

*Time and diet have diminished this delightful occasion.
But, we needn't lose out completely. Most people have all
the pieces necessary to serve an elegant Afternoon Tea and
all the preparation can be done in advance. This is the
only meal where the whole array of food is on view at the
same time. The appetite-appeal of a well thought-out tea
menu knows no challenge, with its abundance of sweet and
savoury foods all deliciously on display.*

Sunday Afternoon Tea at Home

POTTED MEAT

TOMATO SANDWICHES

MUSCATEL BRAN CAKE

ALMOND AND QUINCE SLICES

As a child, the only thing which got me out onto the windswept Yorkshire moors for that walk which was to 'do me so much good', was the visual thought, firmly fixed on the screen of my mind of the tea that would be at the end of the trudge!

These special Sunday trips from the house might be to visit some distant abbey or country house and include a stop at a country tea room. Another monthly event was to accompany my Mama on what we kids called her 'grave galloping', for she truly enjoyed looking round cemeteries where near and distant relatives had been laid to rest. Afterwards we would go back home to a roaring fire and real Afternoon Tea, with potted meat and toast, proper cake and home-made biscuits, things which could be kept for weeks in those handsomely painted biscuit tins, real jam packed with whole strawberries – and – the best tomato sandwiches in the world – well – in Yorkshire perhaps!

POTTED MEAT

MAKES 450 g (1 lb)

450 g (1 lb) boneless and fatless stewing beef
½ cup medium dry Madeira wine or sherry
1 teaspoon salt
1 teaspoon ground mace
1 teaspoon freshly ground black pepper
½ cup clarified butter, cooled

PREPARATION TIME: 30 minutes
COOKING TIME: 3 hours

1 Trim the meat of all skin and fat and cut into 1 cm (½ inch) cubes. Place in a small heatproof bowl or casserole and add the wine and seasonings. Cover tightly with foil and/or a well-fitting lid.

2 Stand the bowl or casserole in a medium saucepan and add boiling water to two-thirds the depth of the pot. Cover and simmer for 2½–3 hours or until the meat is tender. Top up the boiling water as necessary. Remove from the heat and allow to cool.

3 Tip into a liquidizer or food processor and process on top speed until you have a fine purée. With the machine running, gradually add three-quarters of the cool clarified butter. Continue to process until well blended. Taste and adjust the seasoning if necessary.

4 Spoon into 1 large or several individual pots or ramekins. F Spoon over a thin film of the remaining butter completely covering the meat, then chill. Serve with toasted wholemeal bread.

F Freeze for up to 1 month. Thaw overnight in the refrigerator, topping with melted butter when taken from the freezer.

THE NON SOGGY TOMATO SANDWICH

white or brown bread
creamed butter
salt
old fashioned white pepper!
firm but ripe tomatoes (1 per sandwich)

PREPARATION TIME: 10 minutes

Tomato sandwiches with cucumber sandwiches; Almond and quince slices:
Potted meat

1 With a small knife, make a small cross in the base of
each tomato. Plunge them into a pan of boiling water
whilst you count to 20. Remove them into a bowl of cold
water: drain them, then peel off the skins. Butter the bread.

2 Now, this is where the mistake often happens. Most
people slice the tomatoes, I don't. I quarter the
tomatoes, remove the seeds, press the 'petals' flat and lay
them in just one layer on the slice of buttered bread. Add
salt and pepper, press the top on firmly and cut into shapes.

VARIATION
Use cucumber slices sprinkled with salad oil, lemon juice
and salt and pepper.

MUSCATEL BRAN CAKE

225 g (8 oz) bran cereal
225 g (8 oz) seedless muscatel raisins
225 g (8 oz) Barbados sugar
100 g (4 oz) walnuts, roughly chopped
2 teaspoons vanilla essence
450 ml ($\frac{3}{4}$ pint) milk
225 g (8 oz) wholemeal flour
3 teaspoons baking powder

PREPARATION TIME: 20 minutes, plus soaking
COOKING TIME: $1\frac{1}{4}$–$1\frac{1}{2}$ hours
OVEN: 180°C, 350°F, Gas Mark 4

The secret of this wholesome cake is in the flavour of the
muscatel raisins. Serve the cake sliced and well-buttered
together with a mild, crumbly cheese, such as
Wensleydale.

1 Put the bran cereal, raisins, sugar, walnuts and vanilla
essence into a bowl. Cover with the milk and mix well.
Leave to soak for 2 hours.

2 Dredge the flour and baking powder together, then
gradually fold into the fruit and nut mixture. Line a
20 cm (8 inch) square tin with buttered paper, spoon in the
mixture and level the surface. Bake in a preheated oven for
$1\frac{1}{4}$–$1\frac{1}{2}$ hours, until firm to the touch. Leave to cool before
turning out on to a wire tray.

ALMOND AND QUINCE SLICES

MAKES 16–18 SLICES

PÂTE FROLLÉ:
175 g (6 oz) plain flour
75 g (3 oz) unsalted butter, slightly chilled and cubed
75 g (3 oz) caster sugar
1 teaspoon lemon rind
1 egg size 4
25 g (1 oz) ground almonds, sieved
2–3 tablespoons quince or apricot jam

FRANGIPANE:
75 g (3 oz) unsalted butter softened
150 g (5 oz) caster sugar
2 eggs (size 4), at room temperature
1 tablespoon Jamaica rum (optional)
150 g (5 oz) ground almonds
25 g (1 oz) plain white flour
25 g–50 g (1–2 oz) blanched, flaked almonds

PREPARATION TIME: 45 minutes, plus chilling
COOKING TIME: 45 minutes
OVEN: 180°C, 350°F, Gas Mark 4

1 Sift the flour on to the work surface. Make a well in the
centre and add the butter, sugar, lemon rind and egg.
Then add the almonds and 'pinch' together until combined
to a smooth paste. Chill for 30 minutes.

2 Roll out the pastry to line a rectangular tin
30 × 20 × 1 cm (12 × 8 × $\frac{1}{2}$ inch). Chill again before
spreading on the quince or apricot jam.

3 Cream the butter and sugar. Lightly beat the eggs, then
gradually beat into the creamed mixture. Add the rum,
if using, and fold in the almonds and flour. Spread evenly
over the jam base and sprinkle with the almonds.

4 Bake in a preheated oven for 45 minutes. Cut into slices
to serve.

High Tea

SALMON CROQUETTES

FRIED MUSHROOMS AND ONIONS ON TOASTED MUFFINS

YORKSHIRE PLAIT WITH PICKLED WALNUTS

BEEF AND HAM MOULD

CHILLED CREAM COD

To understand how High Tea came into being, you have to know your social history, for this meal, peculiar to the British and still a thriving tradition in some parts of the country, stemmed from the post Industrial Revolution period, and had its roots in the mill and mining areas. Supper was the evening meal for the less well-off up to that point. Dinner was a meal eaten only by the people on the upper rungs of the ladder.

In my home in Yorkshire we only had dinner on Saturdays and Sundays and high days and holidays. High tea, I remember, was a cosy meal, not least because of its informality and the cheerfulness of the table, decked as it was with a gingham cloth thrown over a glowing crimson, bottle-green or ginger brown chenille undercloth bordered with its intricately-knotted fringe. And it was well-suited to a busy working household.

Then, as now, it was a thrifty and easy meal to prepare, for whoever did the cooking could prepare most of it in advance, such as making the breads, biscuits and tea cakes, so that only the main dish had to be prepared on the day. Jams, pickles and chutneys take their place alongside the ham and cheese.

In a nutshell, High Tea could be described as a sort of masculine afternoon tea supplemented with one main dish and perhaps a wedge of cheese, with trifle on Sundays!

My dishes here are in the spirit of High Tea, though remarkably new in concept, and of course can be moved to any part of the day where a tasty dish is required.

SALMON CROQUETTES

SERVES 4

350 g (12 oz) cooked potatoes
25 g (1 oz) butter or 1 tablespoon mayonnaise
1 × 225 g (8 oz) can red salmon, drained
2 hard-boiled eggs, chopped
1 tablespoon roughly chopped fresh parsley
$\frac{1}{4}$ teaspoon mace
1 egg (size 1), beaten
salt
freshly ground black pepper
celery leaves, to garnish

COATING:
2 tablespoons flour
1 egg, beaten
100 g (4 oz) nibbed almonds, or fresh breadcrumbs
olive or soy oil for frying

PREPARATION TIME: 45 minutes, plus chilling
COOKING TIME: 5–10 minutes

1 Mash the potatoes together with the butter or mayonnaise and leave to cool.

2 Loosely mash all the other ingredients in a bowl, add the potatoes and mix well together. Chill for 2 hours until firm.

3 Divide into 8 portions. On a floured work-top, form each portion into a roll or flat croquette. Dredge both sides well with the flour. Dip into the beaten egg and – on a clean plate or kitchen tray – press or roll the almonds or breadcrumbs into each croquette.

4 The mixture is fairly soft, so use a broad-bladed palette knife or fish slice to help move them about. When ready to fry them, heat 5 mm ($\frac{1}{4}$ inch) of oil in a frying pan until smoking. Slide in the croquettes and fry on each side until golden-brown and cooked. Watch them carefully as almonds burn readily. Allow approximately 2–2$\frac{1}{2}$ minutes on each side depending on how thick you have made them.

5 Garnish with celery leaves and serve.

Fried mushrooms and onions on toasted muffins; Salmon croquettes

FRIED MUSHROOMS AND ONIONS ON TOASTED MUFFINS

SERVES 4

350 g (12 oz) white button mushrooms, thinly sliced
1 bunch spring onions
2.5 cm (1 inch) piece green ginger, peeled and finely chopped
2 tablespoons olive or soy oil
salt
freshly ground black pepper
2 teaspoons soy sauce
4 split, toasted muffins, buttered if liked

PREPARATION TIME: 10 minutes
COOKING TIME: 5 minutes

1 Finely slice the mushrooms. Trim and cut the spring onion on a 'long diagonal', almost as thin as the mushrooms. Finely chop the ginger. A

2 Fry the dish in 2 batches. Heat a tablespoon of the oil in a large 25 cm (10 inch) heavy-bottomed pan, until well smoking. Fry half the ginger for 20 seconds or so, working with a straight-edged wooden spatula. Toss in half the mushrooms and fry over a fierce heat, moving them about all the time for about 1 minute. After 30 seconds, add half the onions, seasoning lightly with salt and pepper. The 2 vegetables should retain some of their crispness.

3 Sprinkle over a little of the soy sauce. Stir well and turn into a warm serving dish.

4 Repeat the process for the other half of the ingredients.

5 Serve piled on to hot, split and buttered muffins.

A The vegetables can be prepared in advance and stored overnight in separate bags in the refrigerator.

YORKSHIRE PLAIT WITH PICKLED WALNUTS

SERVES 4–6

2 tablespoons oil or butter
1 medium onion, peeled and finely chopped
4 sticks of celery, washed and diced
1 kg (2 lb) best braising or rump steak, well trimmed and minced
1 tablespoon flour
1 teaspoon ground thyme
1 teaspoon mild curry powder
1 teaspoon sweet paprika
salt
freshly ground black pepper
85 ml (3 fl oz) dry sherry
3 pickled walnuts, diced

PASTRY:
450 g (1 lb) puff pastry, thawed if frozen
flour for dusting
1 egg
top of the milk

PREPARATION TIME: 40 minutes
COOKING TIME: about 1½ hours
OVEN: 200°C, 400°F, Gas Mark 6;
then: 230°C, 450°F, Gas Mark 8;
finally: 190°C, 375°F, Gas Mark 5

Light pastry with a spicy filling makes this a perfect dish for High Tea.

1 To make the filling, heat the oil or butter in a pan, soften the onion and celery over a low-to-medium heat and fry until golden brown.

2 Gradually incorporate the mince and sprinkle over the flour, working in well with a wooden spatula. Add the thyme, curry powder and paprika, 1 teaspoon salt and pepper to taste, then transfer the mixture to a large ovenproof dish.

3 Pour the sherry into the sauces left in the pan and work in well. Add to the mince and leave to cool, stir together well. Ⓐ

4 Cover the dish and cook in a preheated oven for 30 minutes, then add the pickled walnuts. Cool and chill until ready for use.

5 To make the plait, roll out the pastry on a lightly floured board to a rectangle and trim to 30 × 40 cm (12 × 16 inches). Dust with flour and fold lengthways. Put on one side of a wet baking sheet with the fold in the middle. Make a series of 2–3 inch long diagonal cuts at 2 cm (¾ inch) intervals into the longest edges of the rectangle. Unfold the pastry to cover the tray.

6 Brush the pastry all over with egg beaten with a little top of the milk. Spread the cold, stiffish mince mixture down the centre panel of the pastry. Starting at one end, fold the first pair of pastry strips over the filling, overlapping in the centre. Continue in this way until all the filling is encased. Press the pastry strips together.

7 Brush all over with beaten egg, raise the oven temperature and bake for 20 minutes. Reduce the heat and bake for a further 30–35 minutes until the pastry is crisp and golden brown in colour.

8 Serve hot or cold garnished with parsley.

Ⓐ The filling can be made 2–3 days in advance. Cover with cling film and refrigerate.

BEEF & HAM MOULD

MAKES 12–16 SLICES

450 g (1 lb) best braising steak
450 g (1 lb) green gammon
4 slices white bread, made into crumbs
1 heaped teaspoon gelatine crystals
1 level teaspoon ground mace
a little salt if necessary
1 level teaspoon freshly ground black pepper
2 eggs, beaten
1 teacup dry sherry

PREPARATION TIME: 20 minutes
COOKING TIME: 2 hours

This has to be England's most useful member of its 'mould family' for it is delicious served with pickles, or with a well-made salad, or carved thinly as a sandwich filling.

1 Butter a 1–2 litre (2 pint) pudding basin.

2 Trim the steak of all fat. Derind the gammon, retaining the fat. Put both steak and gammon once through the coarse blade of a mincer or mince in a food processor. Mix with the breadcrumbs. Sprinkle over the gelatine crystals and season with salt if necessary and pepper.

3 Bind with the beaten eggs and mix in the sherry.

4 Press the mixture well into the prepared basin, cover with buttered foil, tie down with string and steam over water at a steady rolling boil for 2 hours.

5 Leave to cool. Chill. Turn out of the basin and cut into wedges to serve.

CHILLED CREAM COD

CLOCKWISE FROM THE TOP: Chilled cream cod; Yorkshire plait with pickled walnuts; Beef and ham mould

SERVES 4

½ onion, sliced
150 ml (¼ pint) dry white wine
juice and grated peel of ½ lemon
salt
4–5 peppercorns
750 g (1½ lb) cod fillet, skinned

DRESSING:
150 ml (¼ pint) soured cream
150 ml (¼ pint) single cream
salt
175 g (6 oz) cottage cheese
freshly ground white pepper
squeeze of lemon juice
dash Tabasco sauce

GARNISH:
½ cucumber, peeled, halved, seeded and cut into 5 mm (¼ inch) segments
2 hard-boiled eggs, cut into wedges
chopped fresh green herbs, e.g. dill, parsley, chives
shrimps or prawns

PREPARATION TIME: 40 minutes
COOKING TIME: 15 minutes

1 Place the onion, wine, lemon juice and peel, salt and peppercorns into a saucepan with 300 ml (½ pint) water. Bring to the boil, then simmer for 10 minutes.

2 Cut the cod into pieces, add to the court bouillon, cover and simmer for 5 minutes.

3 Leave to cool in the liquor for 30 minutes. Drain, retaining the liquor. Remove any bones from the fish and flake coarsely with your fingers. Cool completely, then chill, covered with cling film.

4 Using a metal spoon, fold first the soured cream, then the single cream into the cheese. Season well with salt, pepper, lemon juice and the odd dash of Tabasco. If necessary, add a little of the cold cooking liquor to arrive at a loose but not runny consistency.

5 Carefully fold in the chilled fish. Pile the mixture on to a china or glass serving dish and garnish using the ingredients listed. Cover lightly with cling film and chill until ready to serve. Do not leave fish dishes standing in a warm room or outside in the sunshine. A mixed green salad goes well with this dish.

Entertaining Eighteen to Tea

BRIDGE ROLLS WITH POTTED TONGUE AND
POTTED SMOKED TROUT

SCONES

SAUSAGE ROLLS WITH CHICKEN AND PORK
FILLINGS

CURRANT BREAD

RAINBOW CAKE

CHOCOLATE AND ALMOND CAKE

MERINGUES

This is the time to demonstrate in your own home at a traditional time of the day, the very best of British baking. There are delicious rolls spread generously with real potted meat or fish, sausage rolls with crumbling pastry and home-made fillings, miniature scones, warm from the oven with home-made preserves and whipped cream, slices of currant tea bread and a choice of mouth-watering cakes, light meringues and shortbreads.

And this does not need to be restricted to casual entertaining. I would certainly recommend a handsome afternoon tea menu to any hostess who enjoys baking, when she is next confronted with catering for a christening, silver wedding or other special family celebration.

POTTED TONGUE

MAKES 350 g (12 oz)

450 g (1 lb) cooked ox or lamb's tongue
75 g (3 oz) butter
1 tablespoon dark rum
1 teaspoon mild (French) mustard
50 g (2 oz) clarified butter
a few olives and gherkins, to garnish

PREPARATION TIME: 15–20 minutes

1 Cut the tongue into 0.5 cm ($\frac{1}{4}$ inch) thick slices. Cut one slice of tongue into $\frac{1}{2}$ cm ($\frac{1}{4}$ inch) dice.

2 Place the remaining tongue, the butter, rum and mustard into a blender or food processor and blend to a fine paste. Scrape into a bowl and mix in the diced tongue.

3 Spoon into a dish or individual ramekins. F Pour over a thin film of clarified butter, then chill until ready for spreading on bridge rolls (page 21). Garnish and serve.

POTTED SMOKED TROUT

MAKES ABOUT 500 g (1$\frac{1}{4}$ lb)

275 g (10 oz) smoked trout, skinned and boned
75 g (3 oz) butter
100 g (4 oz) full fat soft cheese
2 tablespoons soured cream
juice of $\frac{1}{2}$ small lemon
2–3 dashes Tabasco sauce
$\frac{1}{2}$ teaspoon ground mace
salt
freshly ground black pepper
50 g (2 oz) clarified butter
slices of radish, and cress to garnish

PREPARATION TIME: 15 minutes, plus chilling

1 Purée the trout in a liquidizer or food processor. Add the remaining ingredients, except the butter.

2 Spoon into a pretty dish or individual pots. F Pour over a thin film of clarified butter. Chill to set the butter. Remove from the refrigerator an hour before use. Serve garnished on bridge rolls (page 21).

F Freeze for up to 1 month. Remove, add clarified butter and thaw overnight in the refrigerator.

CLOCKWISE FROM THE TOP: Scones with cream and jam; Bridge rolls with potted tongue and potted smoked trout

SCONES

MAKES 12 SCONES

450 g (1 lb) self-raising flour
½ teaspoon salt
100 g (4 oz) butter
50 g (2 oz) lard
100–175 g (4–6 oz) caster sugar
225 g (8 oz) sultanas
25 g (1 oz) soft, chopped peel
2 eggs (size 1), beaten
150 ml (¼ pint) milk
beaten egg or milk, to glaze.

PREPARATION TIME: 30 minutes
COOKING TIME: 10 minutes
OVEN: 220°C, 425°F, Gas Mark 7

1 Place the baking sheet in the oven to preheat.

2 Sift the flour twice with the salt. Dice the butter and lard into the dry ingredients, then lightly rub in with cool fingertips until the mixture looks like soft bread-crumbs. Mix in the sugar, sultanas and peel. Ⓐ

3 Make a well in the centre and stir in the beaten eggs and half the milk. Add the rest if necessary. Lightly mix with a fork until the ingredients form a soft dough.

4 Turn on to a floured board and knead *very lightly* to a loose, smooth dough. Roll out with a rolling pin or pat with the hand until about 2 cm (¾ inch) thick.

5 Taking care not to twist the cutter, stamp out into 5 cm (2 inch) circles, or cut into triangles with a sharp knife. Lightly knead any trimmings, re-roll and stamp out again.

6 Immediately after shaping, lift with a palette knife on to the hot baking sheet, placing 2.5 cm (1 inch) apart. Brush the tops with lightly beaten egg or milk. Bake towards the top of the preheated oven for about 10 minutes, until well risen and golden brown.

7 Lift on to a cooling rack with the palette knife. Ⓕ Serve split and buttered, then topped with jam and cream.

Ⓕ Freeze for up to 6 months. Thaw for 1–2 hours at room temperature, then warm through in a low oven at 150°C, 300°F, Gas Mark 2.
Ⓐ Can be prepared 1–2 days beforehand, covered with cling film and chilled. Do not mix in the liquid until just before baking.

'SAUSAGE' ROLLS

MAKES 60

450 g (1 lb) plain flour
1 teaspoon salt
175 g (6 oz) butter
50 g (2 oz) lard
1 egg
1 egg yolk
2 tablespoons single cream
milk or beaten egg to glaze

PREPARATION TIME: 1 hour, plus chilling
COOKING TIME: 20–25 minutes
OVEN: 190°C, 375°F, Gas Mark 5

1 Sift the flour and salt into a large bowl. With the finger-tips or a pastry blender, rub in the butter and lard until you have a moist, sand-like texture.

2 Whisk together the egg, egg yolk and cream. Using a fork, mix into the dry ingredients to form a soft dough. With the fingers draw into a ball, wrap in cling film and chill for at least 1 hour.

3 Prepare the fillings (see opposite). Cut the pastry into 2. Roll one half into a rectangle 50 × 30 cm (20 × 12 inches). Cut in half lengthways to give 2 oblongs 50 × 12.5 cm (20 × 5 inches). Place 1 roll of chicken filling down the centre of each pastry oblong. Brush the edges with milk or beaten egg and fold over to enclose the filling. Press and pinch the edges together. F Cut each roll in half and place all 4 rolls on a lightly greased baking sheet. Brush all over with milk or beaten egg and make cuts three-quarters of the way through at approximately 2.5 cm (1 inch) intervals.

4 Repeat with the other half of the pastry and the pork filling. Bake in a preheated oven for 20–25 minutes or until golden brown. Allow to cool slightly before cutting through completely.

F Freeze the rolls shaped but unbaked for up to 2 months. Cook from frozen as above, allowing 5–10 minutes longer. Brush with milk or beaten egg before cooking. They also freeze well cooked; thaw and gently reheat.

Currant bread; Sausage rolls

CHICKEN FILLING

450 g (1 lb) raw, boned chicken breast, skinned and diced
225 g (8 oz) raw ham, diced
100 g (4 oz) streaky bacon, roughly chopped
1 egg
4 tablespoons double cream
50 g (2 oz) fresh white breadcrumbs
1 teaspoon ground mace
1 teaspoon salt
1 teaspoon freshly ground black pepper
4 tablespoons finely chopped fresh parsley

1 Place the chicken, ham and bacon in a food processor or blender and process until fine. Beat the egg with the cream and add to the meat with the breadcrumbs, mace, salt and pepper. Blend thoroughly, finally adding the parsley quickly.

2 Turn on to a floured board, halve and shape each half into a sausage shape which is approximately 50 cm (20 inches) long.

PORK FILLING:

500 g (1¼ lb) boneless pork loin, diced
1 eating apple, preferably a Cox's Orange Pippin, quartered
and peeled
50 g (2 oz) fresh white breadcrumbs
2 teaspoons rubbed sage
½ teaspoon ground mace
1 teaspoon salt
1 teaspoon freshly ground black pepper
1 egg
1 tablespoon double cream

1 Place the pork in a blender or liquidizer and process until finely cut. Slice in the apple, blend for 1 minute, add the remaining ingredients and continue to process just to blend well together.

2 Turn on to a floured board, halve and shape each half into a sausage shape which is approximately 50 cm (20 inches) long.

CURRANT BREAD

MAKES TWO 450 g (1 lb) LOAVES

1 tablespoon dried or 15 oz fresh yeast
1 teaspoon caster sugar
450 ml (¾ pint) warm milk
550 g (1¼ lb) strong plain flour
2 teaspoons salt
25 g (1 oz) lard
225 g (8 oz) currants
25 g (1 oz) peel

GLAZE:
1 tablespoon caster sugar
1 tablespoon milk

PREPARATION TIME: 25 minutes plus proving
COOKING TIME: 45–55 minutes
OVEN: 230°C, 450°F, Gas Mark 8
then: 190°C, 375°F, Gas Mark 5

Delicious served thinly sliced and buttered, with the added luxury of home-made jam or with honey. If any stays around long enough to lose its freshness – which is doubtful – it is equally good toasted.

1 Grease two 450 g (1 lb) loaf tins. Mix the yeast and sugar with two-thirds of the milk and leave in a warm place for about 10 minutes or until frothy.

2 Sift the flour and salt into a large bowl and, with the fingertips, rub in the lard. Mix in the currants and peel, then stir in the yeast mixture and enough of the remaining milk to give a soft dough.

3 Turn out on to a lightly floured surface and knead for about 5 minutes or until firm and elastic. Place in an oiled plastic bag and leave in a warm place for about 1–1½ hours or until the dough has doubled in volume.

4 Punch back and knead again for 5 minutes, then divide into 2 pieces. Shape to fit the loaf tins and place inside. Slip the tins back into the oiled plastic bag and leave to rise for about 20–30 minutes or until the dough has risen to the top of the tins.

5 Bake in a preheated oven for about 15 minutes.

6 Stir the milk and sugar for the glaze together and brush on the tops of the loaves. Reduce the temperature and continue to bake for a further 30–40 minutes. Turn out on to a wire tray to cool. F

F Freeze for up to 1 month. Thaw for 2–3 hours at room temperature.

RAINBOW CAKE

350 g (12 oz) unsalted butter
350 g (12 oz) caster sugar
6 eggs
350 g (12 oz) self-raising flour
2 teaspoons baking powder
25 g (1 oz) ground almonds
2–3 tablespoons milk or water
2–3 drops cochineal
2 teaspoons essence de framboise (optional)
1 tablespoon cocoa powder
grated rind of 1 lemon
1–2 drops yellow food colouring
1 teaspoon almond essence or essence de pistache
1–2 drops green food colouring
2 teaspoons redcurrant jelly
icing sugar, to dredge

PREPARATION TIME: 50 minutes
COOKING TIME: about 1 hour 10 minutes
OVEN: 190°C, 375°F, Gas Mark 5
then: 180°C, 350°F, Gas Mark 4

A marble cake with moist redcurrant jelly running through the marbling.

1 Butter and line a 30 × 10 × 10 cm (12 × 4 × 4 inch) oblong cake tin. Cream the butter and sugar thoroughly. Beat the eggs and fold into the creamed mixture gradually, adding a little of the flour if it shows any sign of curdling.

2 Sift the flour and baking powder together, then fold thoroughly into the mixture, adding the ground almonds as you go along. Add 2–3 tablespoons of milk or water in order to arrive at a loose dropping consistency. Divide the mixture into 3–4 equal parts, depending on whether you want 3 or 4 colours.

3 To the first part add 2–3 drops of cochineal and 2 teaspoons essence de framboise, if using. To the second beat in the cocoa powder. To the third add the lemon rind and 1–2 drops yellow food colouring. To the fourth, add the almond essence and 1–2 drops green food colouring.

4 To make the cake, spoon small amounts of different colours along the bottom of the prepared tin. Give the tin a sharp bang on the worktop to settle things in. Add tiny amounts of the jelly right down the centre. Continue adding the mixture until it is used up but do not put jelly on the top.

5 Bake in a preheated oven for 30 minutes, then reduce the heat and continue baking for a further 35–40 minutes or until cooked. Test with a clean skewer, which should come out clean when inserted in the centre of the cake. Dredge the cake with icing sugar when cold.

CHOCOLATE AND ALMOND CAKE

5 eggs, separated
225 g (8 oz) unsalted butter
225 g (8 oz) caster sugar
225 g (8 oz) plain chocolate
75 g (3 oz) self-raising flour
100 g (4 oz) ground almonds

ICING:
2 tablespoons Maraschino or other fruit liqueur
2 tablespoons water
175 g (6 oz) icing sugar, sieved
50 g (2 oz) cocoa powder, sieved

PREPARATION TIME: 45 minutes
COOKING TIME: 1¼ hours
OVEN: 180°C, 350°F, Gas Mark 4

1 Butter a 23 × 9 cm (9 × 3½ inch) loose-bottomed cake tin generously and line with paper.

2 Cream the egg yolks, butter and sugar together. Break the chocolate into squares and melt in a basin over a pan of hot water off the heat.

3 Sieve the flour and almonds together. Stiffly beat the egg whites until they stand in peaks.

4 Pour the melted chocolate into the egg yolk mixture, then fold in the flour and almonds. Add one third of the egg whites to this mixture and mix in thoroughly, then lightly but again thoroughly, fold in the remainder. Pour the mixture into the prepared tin and bake in a preheated oven for 1¼ hours. The cake is baked when the top is firm to the touch and when, if you listen to it, it is almost silent. Turn on to a tray to cool, then remove the lining paper.

5 To make the icing, gently warm the liqueur taking care it does not ignite. Mix the icing sugar and cocoa powder together. Incorporate the liquid to make a spreadable but stiffish icing, then, using a hot wetted knife, spread a thick cushion of icing on top of the cake.

MERINGUES

MAKES 6–8 PAIRS

4 large egg whites
about 225 g (8 oz) caster sugar (the same weight as the whites)
whipped cream and strawberries, to serve

PREPARATION TIME: 10 minutes
COOKING TIME: 3–4 hours
OVEN: 120°C, 250°F, Gas Mark ½

Chocolate and almond cake; Rainbow cake; Meringues

To make successful meringues, bear the following in mind: The whisk or beaters and the bowl used must be absolutely clean, free from any grease, and dry. Ideally use egg-whites from 2–3 day old eggs that are at room temperature. Be very careful when separating to avoid even the slightest trace of yolk in the whites. Use superfine sugar or equal quantities of superfine and powdered sugar. Line the baking sheet with waxed or nonstick paper.

1 Line the baking sheet.

2 Whisk the egg whites until stiff in a large bowl. Sprinkle over half the sugar and continue to whisk until the texture is smooth and close and stands in stiff peaks when the whisk is removed. Lightly fold in the remaining sugar with a metal spoon.

3 Using a metal spoon and spatula, spoon into ovals on the baking sheet. Alternatively spoon the meringue into a nylon icing bag fitted with a large star nozzle and pipe into cone shapes.

4 Bake in a preheated oven for 3–4 hours or until dry. Cool on a wire tray. Ⓐ Sandwich together with whipped cream and, if liked, fruit, shortly before serving.

Ⓐ Meringues will keep for up to a week, stored in an airtight container.

Cocktails

A drinks party is probably the simplest way of
entertaining in numbers. Some people see it as an easy
way of repaying hordes of owed invitations – a situation
which cannot always be avoided in life. Others, like me,
find it a useful way of seeing family and friends for a
couple of hours more frequently than if we waited to find a
convenient time to meet up for an evening meal.
Some of the nibbles can be chosen from a selection of
things which will freeze, and much of the preparation for
the rest can be done in advance. You can make as many or
as few of the varieties as you choose, following the
suggestions for balancing hot and cold food.
Read through recipes here and I think you'll quickly find
an excuse to have a couple of dozen pals round for drinks.

The Crudités Party

The vast banks of fresh fruit and vegetables filling the market squares and side streets of the South of France, and Provence in particular, are one of the abiding memories of visits to that part of the world.

On the first occasion it came as something of a shock to discover that they were meant to be eaten raw and dipped into thick garlic-ridden mayonnaise to boot! Not only that but the radishes were accompanied by a slab of butter. But, that is where the idea of serving crudités began. Things have changed somewhat since then, not least because some of us have travelled to the United States where things are done differently, and to my thinking, better.

The crudité party is one area where you can manifest your personal style to great effect – but at not too great a cost – particularly if you are entertaining a large number of people. For now you can bring out those vast meat platters; now you can completely cover a kitchen table top with green and red cabbage leaves; or you can line tea trays, shallow baskets and wicker trays with ferns and rustic leaves, garland them with wreaths of pretty flower heads and pile them high with multi-coloured mosaics of fresh vegetables with their attendant sauces nearby.

There is almost nothing we cannot get in Britain today *but* things must now be treated differently from the far-off 1950s when crudités first came to England. I would like you to take a look at crudités in a different light.

I divide the many vegetables available to us into different categories, depending on their treatment. Some I ask you to blanch in aromatic stocks, acidulated waters, even fruit juices, to give them more colour and more appetite appeal without losing that all-essential crispness. Others I suggest you serve in huge bowls of cracked ice to keep them cool and crisp, yet others are to be spiked with a long, strong bamboo skewer for ease of dipping and safety of manoeuvring. The dips too are carefully prepared to complement the natural vegetable flavours.

In choosing your vegetables it is crucial to select carefully: look for the youngest, smallest and freshest produce. Then trim, clean, wash, blanch and store them in separate plastic bags to prevent cross-flavouring, whilst they await their turn to be dressed.

There are, however, some vegetables which do not lend themselves to the crudité platters, such as aubergines, okra, artichokes (unless you are using their cooked hearts), pumpkins, courgettes which are not ideal, and turnips which are forbidden as they tend to be indigestible.

Of those vegetables which do, here is my table of how to prepare them. When calculating overall quantities, allow 75–100 g (3–4 oz) of vegetables per person; 600 ml (1 pint) of dip will serve 12–14 people. All vegetables should be well drained on layers of paper towels for 30 minutes. Store in airtight containers or sealed plastic bags in the refrigerator. All can be prepared a day ahead.

VEGETABLES

1 Vegetables which are best left completely raw and are of a size which need neither cutting nor shaping:

Belgian endive – serve in spikes fanned out in a bowl of crushed ice.

Button mushrooms – serve, spiked with a cocktail stick in acidulated, iced water.

Cherry tomatoes – pull out the stalk and spike on a long bamboo skewer.

Radishes – leave an inch of the green top on. Serve in a container of iced water.

Sugar peas or Mange tout – string if necessary, split and fill with soft cheese or leave whole. Serve over crushed ice.

2 Vegetables used completely raw and for special cutting:

Celery – trim, clean, break into blades then cut into sticks. Serve on cracked ice or in iced water.

Cucumbers – peeling is optional. Cut in half lengthways. Scoop out the seeds. Cut in 1 cm ($\frac{1}{2}$ inch) strips, then into 4–5 cm (2 inch) pieces. Store in an airtight container. They will appear to dehydrate somewhat, but this doesn't matter.

Fennel – as for celery.

Peppers, green, red and yellow – cut in half. Shake out the seeds. Cut away excess ribs of white pith. Cut into sticks or petals. Serve on cracked ice.

Spring onions – trim. Leave an inch of green on. Cut in half lengthways. Serve on cracked ice.

3 Vegetables for blanching:

Asparagus tips – choose young thin stems. Cut into 5 cm (2 inch) pieces. You should get 3 per stem. Blanch as for cauliflower florets.

Brussels sprouts – select and trim the tiniest possible, ideally 1 cm ($\frac{1}{2}$ inch) in diameter. Cut larger ones in half. Blanch as for cauliflower.

Carrots – peel, wash and cut into batons 5 cm ($\frac{1}{4}$ inch) square by 4 cm ($1\frac{1}{2}$ inches) long, or 3 mm ($\frac{1}{8}$ inch) thick × 1 cm ($\frac{1}{2}$ inch) wide by 5 cm (2 inches) long. Blanch in a mixture of orange juice and chicken stock (half and half) for $\frac{1}{2}$ minute only. Cool, chill.

Cauliflower florets – break and cut into 1 cm ($\frac{1}{2}$ inch) florets. Blanch for 1 minute in boiling, salted water or strained chicken stock to retain their whiteness. Rinse under cold running water. Drain. Spike with a cocktail stick.

Green beans – top and tail them. Cut into 5 cm (2 inch) lengths. Blanch as for cauliflower.

4 Completely cooked vegetables (not strictly crudités but can be included):

Beetroots – Peel cooked beetroots and scoop into balls with a 1.5 cm ($\frac{3}{4}$ inch) melon baller. Serve away from other vegetables to avoid staining.

Mini new potatoes – select the tiniest possible and of an even size. Cook in chicken stock. Toss in a drop of olive oil. Dredge lightly with mace or nutmeg.

IDEAS FOR PRESENTATION

Large peppers – Cut the top off 1 cm ($\frac{1}{2}$ inch) down. Cut and scoop out the seeds and pith 'ribs'. Use to hold dips.

Red and Savoy cabbages – Cut out enough of the heart to make a hollow large enough to contain whichever vegetables you have decided upon. Leave the good-looking, outer leaves attached and store the cabbage in a bucket of cold water until ready for filling.

THE DIPS

GARLIC MAYONNAISE
To each 600 ml (1 pint) of mayonnaise (page 23) add:
6 garlic cloves, crushed

HERB MAYONNAISE
To each 600 ml (1 pint) of home-made mayonnaise (page 23) add:
2 tablespoons finely snipped fresh chives
1 tablespoon finely chopped fresh parsley
1 tablespoon finely chopped fresh basil or tarragon

PARSLEY AND ANCHOVY MAYONNAISE
To each 600 ml (1 pint) of home-made mayonnaise (page 23) add:
2 sieved hard-boiled egg yolks
8 anchovy fillets, finely chopped
2 tablespoons chopped fresh parsley
the oil from the anchovies
1 heaped teaspoon mild French mustard
1 garlic clove, crushed

MUSHROOM AND SHERRY MAYONNAISE
225 g (8 oz) flat cap (dark) mushrooms, roughly chopped
1 teacup Amontillado sherry
1 teaspoon mild French mustard
50 ml (2 fl oz) chicken stock (use ¼ stock cube)
450 ml (¾ pint) home-made mayonnaise (page 23)

1 Simmer all the ingredients together in a small pan for 10–15 minutes. Remove the mushrooms with a slotted spoon and reduce the remaining liquid by boiling rapidly to 2 tablespoons of strong essence.

2 Make a purée of the cooked, cool mushrooms, then mix this and the essence into the mayonnaise.

DILL DIP
Mix together:
450 g (1 lb) cottage cheese, squeezed
juice of 1 lemon
1 tablespoon grated onion
2 dashes Tabasco sauce
2 tablespoons finely chopped dill fronds
freshly ground white pepper

SOUR CREAM DIP
To each 600 ml (1 pint) of soured cream add:
2 tablespoons, squeezed and chopped capers
2 tablespoons finely snipped chives
2 tablespoons chopped apple or ginger mint
salt
freshly ground white pepper

SMOKED SALMON AND YOGURT DIP
To each 600 ml (1 pint) whisked plain unsweetened yogurt add:
175 g (6 oz) smoked salmon, finely chopped
salt sparingly
1 small bunch spring onions, trimmed and very finely sliced

HAZELNUT AND YOGURT DIP
To each 600 ml (1 pint) plain unsweetened yogurt or sour cream add:
175 g (6 oz) lightly toasted and finely crushed hazelnuts
⅛ teaspoon cayenne pepper
salt sparingly

Small Cocktail Food for Fifty

COLD DISHES

CUCUMBER CUPS WITH TARAMASALATA

DEVILLED TONGUE CANAPÉS

GRAVADLAX ON RYE BREAD

BUTTERY CHEDDAR SHORTBREADS

CURRIED STUFFED PRUNES

HERB MARINATED LEEKS

APPLE SLICES WITH CHICKEN LIVER PÂTÉ

HOT DISHES

GRILLED WATER CHESTNUTS WRAPPED IN BACON

SPICED SAUSAGES IN PASTRY WRAPS

For a 2 hour party from 11 a.m.–1 p.m. or 5 p.m.–7 p.m. you will need to allow 4 of the richer pieces per head, i.e. 200 canapés in all, plus bowls of cheese straws, good large olives, plain crackers or small salted pretzels and salted cashews, pecans or almonds.

Choose to serve 2 hot or warm savouries and 3 or 4 cold varieties.

Have all the fillings, tartlet cases, biscuits for holding fillings and toppings ready the day before. Breads and biscuits can be ready spread with butter or whatever and stored in papered layers in air-tight containers.

If you are having a pre-theatre or concert drinks party, then you might perhaps like to include one or two of the more substantial savouries from the American Cocktails (pages 90 to 97). A lot of the recipes there are obviously interchangeable; it is simply a matter of 'cutting-things-down-to-size'.

Hot canapés and savouries should be served one variety to a dish. Cold varieties can be arranged on attractive platters, lined with a linen napkin, in rows, circles or just in an attractive mosaic of shape, texture and colour.

CUCUMBER CUPS WITH TARAMASALATA

MAKES ABOUT 60

10 slices white or brown bread
225–275 g (8–10 oz) taramasalata
2 small cucumbers, peeled
8 tomatoes, about 750 g ($1\frac{1}{2}$ lb), skinned, seeded and chopped
8 basil leaves, finely chopped
salt
freshly ground black pepper

PREPARATION TIME: 35 minutes

1 Using a pastry cutter the same diameter as the cucumbers, cut out approximately 60 circles of bread. Ⓐ Spread each with taramasalata.

2 Cut each cucumber into 25–30 × 8 mm ($\frac{1}{3}$ inch) discs. Using a corer or small pastry cutter, or a pointed knife, cut out the seeds and discard. Ⓐ

3 Sit a ring of cucumbers on top of each circle of bread. Mix the tomato with the basil and season with salt and pepper. Ⓐ Use the tomato mixture to fill the centre of the cucumber rings.

Ⓐ The circles of bread can be made the day before, and the cucumber can be cut and the tomato filling made. Assemble on the day used.

DEVILLED TONGUE CANAPÉS

MAKES 40–50

225 g (8 oz) tongue, cubed
1 teaspoon French mustard
1 tablespoon Worcestershire sauce
1 tablespoon fruit chutney

TO SERVE:
40–50 cheese biscuits or circles of buttered bread
salted almonds, halved stuffed olives or pearl onions

PREPARATION TIME: 20 minutes

1 Place all the ingredients in a liquidizer or food processor and process to a smooth paste. Spread on the biscuits or bread.

2 Top with a salted almond, a half stuffed olive or a pearl onion.

CLOCKWISE FROM THE TOP: Devilled tongue canapés with curried stuffed prunes; Buttery cheddar shortbreads; Gravadlax on rye bread

GRAVADLAX ON RYE BREAD

MAKES 60

225 g (8 oz) butter, softened
1 scant teaspoon honey
2 teaspoons French mustard
2 teaspoons lemon juice
1 tablespoon finely chopped dill weed or 1 teaspoon dried dill
salt
freshly ground black pepper
1 packet light Danish rye bread, or German Vollkorubrot
(approx. 10 slices)
350 g (12 oz) gravadlax or smoked salmon
jar capers or dill weed or half green pepper, to garnish

PREPARATION TIME: 30 minutes

1 Using a palette knife work the butter on top of a large dinner plate or clean work surface until it is readily spreadable. Make a hollow and put in the honey, mustard, lemon juice, dill weed and season with salt and plenty of pepper. Work all these into the butter thoroughly, then scrape into a basin.

2 Lay 10 slices of rye bread flat on the work surface. Spread liberally with the savoury butter. **A**

3 Cover with thin slices of whichever salmon you are using. Cut each slice of bread in half lengthways, then across into 3, yielding 6 small oblong pieces. Decorate each piece with a small sprig of fresh dill weed, a few capers, or a thinly sliced bit of green pepper. Chill until ready to serve.

A The rye bread slices can be buttered 2–3 days in advance and stored with a piece of paper or cling film between each slice and wrapped in cling film. Unwrap the whole stack and cover with the salmon just before serving.

BUTTERY CHEDDAR SHORTBREADS

MAKES 70–80

225 g (8 oz) dryish mature Cheddar cheese
225 g (8 oz) cold butter, cubed
225 g (8 oz) plain white flour
salt
freshly ground black pepper
tip of a pointed knife cayenne pepper

PREPARATION TIME: 30 minutes
COOKING TIME: 10 minutes per batch
OVEN: 190°C, 375°F, Gas Mark 5

1 Grate the cheese on the coarse, spike-tooled side of a grater (not the half-moon teeth). Rub the butter into the flour until you have a sand-like texture, adding $\frac{1}{4}$ teaspoon salt and pepper as you go along and sprinkling over the modicum of cayenne pepper. Using a large fork, thoroughly mix in the grated cheese. The dough will be a bit sticky to handle.

2 Lightly butter 2 large baking sheets. Lightly flour a work top. Cut or scoop up half-teaspoons of the mixture and roll them into even-sized balls. You should get between 70–80. Arrange the balls in rows on the baking trays. Dip the tines of a fork in flour and press each biscuit each way, flattening to a round 4 cm ($1\frac{1}{2}$ inches) in diameter, leaving the criss-cross marks across the top.

3 Bake in a preheated oven for 8–10 minutes, or until golden and crisp right through. Leave to cool for 15 minutes before attempting to remove them to a wire tray with a palette knife. They are fragile. Leave to cool completely. If they are even modestly uncooked inside, return the tray to the oven for a few more minutes. **A**

A Can be made up to 1 week in advance. Store in an airtight container in layers, and with layers of soft paper towels between. Store in a cool, *dry* place. In summer butter and cheese soon go rancid if not stored properly.

CURRIED STUFFED PRUNES

MAKES 50

50 giant prunes
strong tea, to cover
25 g (1 oz) butter
50 g (2 oz) onion, finely chopped
$1\frac{1}{2}$ teaspoons curry paste
1 tablespoon tomato purée
1 teaspoon muscovado sugar
2 tablespoons brandy
$\frac{1}{4}$ teaspoon salt
freshly ground black pepper
450 g (1 lb) full fat soft cheese
50 walnut halves, salted (see below)

PREPARATION TIME: 45 minutes, plus soaking overnight
COOKING TIME: 10 minutes

To salt the walnuts, scatter the walnuts on an oven tray. Heat through in the oven at 160°C, 325°F, Gas Mark 3 for a few minutes. Remove and salt lightly. Cool before using.

1 Soak the prunes in strong tea for 3 hours or overnight, then split and pit them.

2 Melt the butter in a small pan, add the onion and fry until golden brown. Stir in the curry paste and tomato purée and cook for a few seconds, stirring continuously. Add the sugar and brandy, then season with the salt and some pepper.

3 Cook for a further 10–15 seconds, then cool and rub through a sieve.

4 Beat the cheese until smooth, then beat in the curry purée. Fill a piping bag fitted with a plain 1 cm ($\frac{1}{2}$ inch) tube. Pipe some of the mixture into each prune. Top with a salted walnut.

HERB MARINATED LEEKS

MAKES ABOUT 50

12 × 2.5 cm (1 inch) diameter leeks
1 × 150 ml ($\frac{1}{4}$ pint) carton plain unsweetened yogurt
1 tablespoon rich olive oil
2 tablespoons lemon juice, strained
1 teaspoon mild French mustard
1 teaspoon caster sugar
salt
freshly ground black pepper
4 tablespoons mixed fresh herbs, using chives, basil,
marjoram, tarragon, dill weed and/or fennel seed
900 ml (1$\frac{1}{2}$ pints) chicken stock to cover (made from stock
cubes)
lettuce leaves (1 cos lettuce), to serve

PREPARATION TIME: 30 minutes, plus draining and
cooling overnight
COOKING TIME: 2 minutes

1 Cut the leeks into 2.5 cm (1 inch) pieces, about 4 per
leek, and soak in cold water for an hour to clean. Drain.

2 Place the yogurt, oil, lemon juice, mustard, sugar, salt
and pepper into a large screw-top jar and shake until
smooth and creamy. Transfer to a 2.25 litre (4 pint) bowl
and mix.

3 Bring the stock to a fast boil, tip in the leeks and cook
for only 2 minutes. Drain (retaining the stock for soup
or gravy) and cool overnight in a plastic colander, so that
any excess water is drained away. Toss in the herb
marinade to cool completely.

4 To serve, stand each leek on a little lettuce leaf saucer.
Spike through with a cocktail stick.

APPLE SLICES WITH CHICKEN LIVER PÂTÉ

MAKES APPROX. 50

3 Cox's apples
juice of 1 lemon, strained
225 g (8 oz) chicken liver pâté
50 capers
50 salted peanuts

PREPARATION TIME: 30 minutes

1 Core the apples, then cut in half and again into quarters.
Cut each quarter into wedges. Toss the wedges in the
lemon juice to prevent discoloration.

2 Beat the pâté until soft and smooth. Fill a piping bag
fitted with a 1 cm ($\frac{1}{2}$ inch) ribbon tube with the pâté
and pipe ribbons on to each apple slice. Top with a caper
and a peanut.

GRILLED WATER CHESTNUTS, WRAPPED IN BACON

MAKES 50

1 tablespoon soy sauce
1 tablespoon olive oil
$\frac{1}{2}$ teaspoon ground mace
1 clove garlic, crushed
2–3 dashes Tabasco sauce
50 water chestnuts, rinsed and drained (3–4 225 g (8 oz)
cans)
17 long rashers, rinded, streaky bacon
oil for brushing

PREPARATION TIME: 30 minutes, plus marinating
overnight
COOKING TIME: 4 minutes per batch

1 Mix the soy sauce, oil, mace, garlic and Tabasco
together in a basin.

2 Prick each chestnut through once or twice, then toss in
the marinade, cover with cling film and leave for 2
hours or overnight. Drain if necessary, though all the
marinade should have been absorbed.

3 Cut each bacon rasher diagonally into 3 pieces. Wrap a
piece round each chestnut and secure with a wooden
pick or cocktail stick.

4 Brush the grill pan with a little oil and grill the wrapped
chestnuts under a high heat for 2 minutes on each side
or until the bacon is crisp.

SPICED SAUSAGES IN PASTRY WRAPS

CLOCKWISE FROM THE TOP: Spiced sausages in pastry wraps; Apple slices with chicken liver; Grilled water chestnuts, wrapped in bacon

MAKES 50

2 × 350 g (12 oz) packets frozen shortcrust or puff pastry,
thawed
50 chipolata sausages
1 tablespoon French mustard
1 tablespoon tomato purée
1 tablespoon olive oil
1 egg (size 1) beaten with 2 tablespoons cream cr top of the
milk
50 g (2 oz) sesame seeds

PREPARATION TIME: 30 minutes
COOKING TIME: 15 minutes per batch
Oven: 200°C, 400°F, Gas Mark 6

1 Roll out the pastry 3 mm ($\frac{1}{8}$ inch) thick. Cut into 2.5 cm (1 inch) wide strips and cut each strip into a length long enough to wrap round the waist of each sausage – measure with a piece of paper first.

2 Mix the mustard, tomato purée and oil together in a large bowl. Toss the raw sausages in this to coat thinly.

3 Wrap a piece of pastry round the waist of each sausage, seal and brush lightly with the beaten egg mixture. Dip the ends into the sesame seeds.

4 Place in rows on lightly buttered baking sheets and bake in a preheated oven for approximately 10–15 minutes. Serve hot or cold.

American Cocktail Food

In this section we are concerned with 'more than a canapé yet not quite a buffet'. We are talking of finger food of a more substantial nature. Food of a nature which will satisfy the hungry but can be almost ignored by the fed! With this type of food, the style of presentation is quite different from the mosaics of miniscule savouries you would serve on another occasion.

Huge platters, wide trays, flat shallow baskets, even trugs come into their own; which you then line with attractive napkins (no paper doilys please), fronds of rinsed ferns and brackens, large flat vine leaves, straw, even cushions of moss or – dare I say it – plastic grass – and at Christmas time a cluster of baubles. This is the only embellishment needed to make perfect platforms for your food.

Serve only one type of savoury on each tray. This makes life easier for your guests, as their concentrated conversation is not interrupted by having to peer at a confusing selection. It also makes life easier in the kitchen as you can replenish each tray elegantly as it empties.

For roughly a dozen people, serve 2–3 dishes combining hot and cold food; for 25–30 people a choice from 4–5 hot and cold dishes could be offered.

The trays should be large enough also to contain a small pile of cocktail-sized finger napkins, in case anyone should wish to wipe their fingers.

★ Recipes marked with an asterisk make good starters for a dinner menu.

COLD DISHES

MINIATURE BEEF TARTARES ON PUMPERNICKEL

SPICED CRAB-STUFFED EGGS

COLD SAVOURY OMELETTES WITH PROSCIUTTO AND MELON

MANGE TOUT WITH JUMBO PRAWNS★

BACON SCONES WITH CHEESE★

MEAT-STUFFED CHERRY TOMATOES WITH BASIL

Spiced crab-stuffed eggs; Miniature beef tartares on bread

MINIATURE BEEF TARTARES ON PUMPERNICKEL

MAKES 24–32 PIECES

3 peppers (if possible 1 yellow, 1 red, 1 green)
1 large onion, sliced
olive oil
butter
750 g (1½ lb) fillet of beef, minced
1 tablespoon chopped fresh parsley
juice of 1 lemon
salt
freshly ground black pepper
6–8 slices pumpernickel or Danish rye bread
parsley sprigs, to garnish

PREPARATION TIME: 30 minutes, plus cooling
COOKING TIME: 30 minutes

1 Clean and slice the peppers. Put them into a frying pan together with the onion, some olive oil and a knob of butter. Fry gently until both the peppers and the onions are cooked and tender, approximately 30 minutes. Allow to cool and chop finely.

2 Mix these vegetables with the minced meat, adding some olive oil, the parsley, lemon juice, salt and pepper, according to taste.

3 Spread the mixture thickly on the slices of bread, then cut each piece into 4. Top each one with a tiny sprig of parsley.

VARIATION
This tartare is also good served on small Bath Oliver biscuits or small water biscuits.

SPICED CRAB-STUFFED EGGS

MAKES 20 PIECES

10 hard-boiled eggs

FILLING:
175 g (6 oz) butter, softened
1 × 275 g (10 oz) dressed crab weighed after dressing (or use frozen light and dark meat)
50 g (2 oz) freshly grated Parmesan cheese
1½ heaped teaspoons tarragon or French mustard
1 garlic clove, crushed
2 good dashes Tabasco sauce
scant teaspoon salt
good squeeze lemon juice
2 heaped teaspoons tomato purée
1 tablespoon chopped fresh tarragon (or parsley)
1 teaspoon pepper

TO SERVE:
4–6 slices bread
fresh tarragon

PREPARATION TIME: 20 minutes
COOKING TIME: 10 minutes (for the eggs)

1 Cut the eggs in half lengthways. Take out the yolks.

2 Put the yolks with all the other filling ingredients into a blender or food processor and blend until smooth. Rub through a fine-meshed sieve. Put the mixture into a piping bag fitted with a large rose nozzle, then pipe the mixture into the eggs.

3 Cut circles, 4 cm (1½ inches) in diameter from the bread and toast lightly. Sit each half egg on a circle of bread and top each one with a sprig of tarragon.

COLD SAVOURY OMELETTES WITH PROSCIUTTO AND MELON

MAKES 24

3 eggs (size 2)
2 teaspoons plain flour
2 tablespoons single cream or top of the milk
salt
freshly ground black pepper
a little soy oil for frying

FILLING:
1 small ripe melon
juice of 1 lemon, strained
dredge of ginger
12 thin slices Parma ham

PREPARATION TIME: 30 minutes
COOKING TIME: 30–40 minutes

1 Place the eggs, flour, cream or milk and salt and pepper into a blender or into a jug just wide enough to take a rotary whisk, and blend or whisk together. If not in a jug, now pour into one.

2 Heat a teaspoon of soy oil in a 15 cm (6 inch) frying pan until smoking. Pour away the oil into a cup and lower the heat. Pour in just enough of the omelette mixture to coat the bottom of the pan as you swirl it around. As soon as it is set, flip the omelette over with a palette knife, leaving it on its other side just those *few* seconds it will take to set.

3 Tip the omelette on to a tray lined with greaseproof paper.

4 Continue, making 5 more omelettes in the same way, raising and lowering the heat as is necessary and adding just a modicum of oil again if needed and pouring off before frying the next omelette.

5 Store the omelettes, as you make them, in stacks and between layers of paper. (Use the day they are made.)

6 Cut the melon in half and scoop out the seeds. Cut each half into 3 long wedges, then cut the flesh away from the skin. Now cut each wedge lengthways across the middle and these portions in half again, lengthways, giving you 24 pointed pieces. Dredge lightly with the lemon juice and ginger. Cut the slices of ham in half across the middle, then wrap a piece of ham round each melon piece.

7 Cut each omelette into quarters. Place each melon piece on a quarter omelette and pull the omelette corners up around the melon. Spear through with a wooden stick. Serve on a china or glass platter with no napkin – perhaps on a bed of picked watercress sprigs. Cover and chill until ready to serve.

MANGE TOUT WITH JUMBO PRAWNS

YIELDS 20 PIECES

2 tablespoons olive oil
2 tablespoons lemon juice
½ teaspoon mild French mustard
1 teaspoon caster sugar
small garlic clove, crushed
1 tablespoon finely chopped fresh dill, chives or parsley
20 cooked jumbo prawns, peeled
20 large even size mange tout, topped and tailed

PREPARATION TIME: 30 minutes, plus marinating
COOKING TIME: 30 seconds

1 Place the oil, lemon juice, mustard, sugar, garlic and herbs in a 2.25 litre (4 pint) bowl and mix well together using a small balloon whisk. Put in the prawns, cover with cling film and leave to marinate, refrigerated, for 2 hours, shaking or turning the prawns from time to time.

2 Cook the peas in boiling, salted water for 30 seconds only. Drain and cool under cold running water. Drain again. Split the peas down one side and separate into 2 pieces, insides up. Remove the prawns from the marinade, lay one across each split pod and fold the pod over the centre of the prawn and secure with a cocktail stick.

BACON SCONES WITH CHEESE

MAKES 16–20 SMALL SCONES

225 g (8 oz) self-raising flour
½ teaspoon salt
freshly ground black pepper
¼ teaspoon ground mace or nutmeg
100 g (4 oz) lard
4 rashers of bacon, chopped, fried until crisp and cooled
2 eggs (size 3 or 4)
2 tablespoons cold water
225 g (8 oz) cottage or full fat soft cheese
chives, to garnish

PREPARATION TIME: 30 minutes
COOKING TIME: 10–12 minutes
OVEN: 190°C, 375°F, Gas Mark 5

1 Season the flour with salt, pepper and mace or nutmeg. Rub in the lard, then add the bacon bits. Beat the eggs with 2 tablespoons of cold water and add to the dry ingredients, binding loosely to form a soft dough.

2 Press the dough out on to a floured board till it reaches 2 cm (¾ inch) in thickness. Cut out scones 4 cm (1½ inches) in diameter.

3 Bake on a buttered baking sheet in a preheated oven for 10–12 minutes.

4 Garnish and serve split and spread with cottage or soft cheese.

MEAT-STUFFED CHERRY TOMATOES WITH BASIL

MAKES 25

1 tablespoon olive oil
100 g (4 oz) bacon, minced
100 g (4 oz) onion, finely chopped
4 white mushrooms, finely chopped
2 tablespoons chopped basil
2 tablespoons parsley, finely chopped
2 teaspoons freshly chopped thyme
1 garlic clove, crushed
salt
freshly ground black pepper
100 g (4 oz) white breadcrumbs, fried until golden-brown in
50 g (2 oz) butter
25 cherry tomatoes
Tabasco sauce
squeeze of lemon juice

PREPARATION TIME: 40 minutes, plus cooling
COOKING TIME: 15–20 minutes
OVEN: 200°C, 400°F, Gas Mark 6

1 Heat the oil, fry the minced bacon until almost crisp, add the onion and fry until soft. Add the mushrooms and soften these too, then mix in all the herbs and garlic. Season well with salt and pepper and finally mix in the breadcrumbs and remove from the heat.

2 Cut the tops off the tomatoes. Using the handle end of a spoon, scoop out all the pips and juice and discard. Season the insides with salt and pepper, the odd dash of Tabasco, and a little squeeze of lemon juice. (It's these touches that count so much in cookery.) Fill the tomatoes with the stuffing and balance the tiny caps on top. Ⓐ

3 Place in a large, well-buttered dish and bake in a preheated oven for 10 minutes, or until really hot right through but not collapsed. Cool, but do not refrigerate.

Ⓐ The tomatoes can be filled the day before and refrigerated. Cook an hour or two before serving, so that they are still very moist.

CLOCKWISE FROM THE TOP: Bacon scones with cheese; Cold savoury omelettes with prosciutto and melon; Meat-stuffed cherry tomatoes with basil; Mange tout with jumbo prawns

HOT DISHES

INDIVIDUAL BOLOGNESE TARTS

BABY SMOKED HADDOCK FISH CAKES

PHYLLO PASTIES WITH SPINACH AND FETA CHEESE

SKEWERS OF SPICED CHICKEN AND PINEAPPLE★

BABY RAREBITS★

HOT ROAST LOIN OF PORK ON HERB BREAD★

★ see page 90

INDIVIDUAL BOLOGNESE TARTLETS

MAKES 20–24

225 g (8 oz) best stewing or rump steak
1 small onion, very finely chopped
1 tablespoon olive oil
40 g (1½ oz) tomato purée
15 g (1½ oz) plain flour
150 ml (¼ pint) red wine
1 garlic clove, crushed
150 ml (¼ pint) stock or water
salt
freshly ground black pepper
20–24 baked 4 cm (1½ inch) tartlet cases (page 16)

GARNISH:
fresh coriander leaves
diamonds of red pepper

PREPARATION TIME: 20 minutes
COOKING TIME: about 1 hour

1 Trim away fat and sinews from the meat and put twice through a mincer or mince in a food processor.

2 Fry the onion in the oil in a heavy-bottomed pan until golden brown. Gradually add the minced meat, stirring well over a good heat until the meat browns. Now reduce the heat and add the tomato purée, taking care to work it well in, making sure that it does not burn. Sprinkle the flour over and mix well.

3 Over a low heat gradually allow a crust to form on the bottom of the pan. This should take about 10 minutes, but watch it carefully. Remove the mixture to a large dinner plate. Turn up the heat again and pour in the red wine. With a wooden spatula work all this crust into a sauce. When the bottom of the pan is quite clear, put the meat mixture back into the winy sauce, add the crushed garlic and the stock or water and simmer for 30 minutes.

4 Season lightly, bearing in mind, if you have used a stock cube, that it already contains salt. Fill the tartlet cases with this mixture and garnish when ready to serve.

BABY SMOKED HADDOCK FISH CAKES

Use the recipe for Haddock Fish Cakes on page 125.

Make them 2.5–4 cm (1–1½ inches) in diameter, and serve hot or cold, spiked on a bamboo skewer with slices of lime, piled in a napkin-lined basket, with a bowl of home-made mayonnaise (page 23) or tartare sauce.

PHYLLO PASTIES WITH SPINACH AND FETA CHEESE

MAKES 18

FILLING:
25 g (1 oz) butter
1 small bunch spring onions, trimmed and finely chopped
1 × 225 g (8 oz) packet frozen leaf spinach, thawed, well-drained and roughly chopped
225 g (8 oz) Feta cheese
salt
freshly ground black pepper
¼ teaspoon nutmeg
1 × 450 g (1 lb) packet phyllo pastry (strudel leaves)
175 g (6 oz) unsalted butter, melted and cooled
sprig of coriander, to garnish

PREPARATION TIME:
COOKING TIME:
OVEN: 200°C, 400°F, Gas Mark 6

Phyllo, or strudel, pastry is bought frozen. Leave it to thaw out in the refrigerator overnight. A 450 g (1 lb) packet will give you approximately 12 sheets or 'leaves' as they are sometimes called.

1 First prepare the filling. Melt the butter in a pan and soften the onion. Add the spinach and just heat through. Leave to cool, then mix in the cheese and season delicately with salt, pepper and the nutmeg.

2 Lay the first leaf or sheet of phyllo carefully on a clean work surface. Brush all over, right to the edges, with melted butter. Lay over a second sheet. Brush this, then a third and a fourth.

3 Cut the sheet across into 6 equal strips (3–3½ inches) wide. Put a heaped teaspoon of your chosen filling on the bottom left-hand corner of each strip. Fold over this corner, so that the bottom edge lies over the right hand side. Now continue to fold this triangle up and over until you get to the top of each strip with a triangular shaped 'parcel'. Brush the triangles all over with more melted butter. Repeat this process twice more, yielding 18 parcels.

4 Place the parcels on a buttered baking sheet and bake in a preheated oven for 12–14 minutes, until golden brown and crisp. Serve hot or cold garnished with coriander.

CLOCKWISE FROM THE TOP: Phyllo pasties with spinach and feta cheese; Individual bolognese tartlets; Baby smoked haddock fish cakes

VARIATIONS
The following can be added to 225 g (8 oz) of seasoned Feta cheese:
1. 225 g (8 oz) smoked salmon, diced
2. 100 g (4 oz) crushed walnuts
3. 100 g (4 oz) crispy fried diced bacon and 100 g (4 oz) fried chopped mushrooms
4. 225 g (8 oz) flaked cooked and filleted kipper and 1 tablespoon capers, drained and roughly chopped

SKEWERS OF SPICED CHICKEN AND PINEAPPLE

MAKES 20 SKEWERS

MARINADE:
2 tablespoons olive oil
1 garlic clove, crushed
1 teaspoon salt
1 teaspoon freshly ground black pepper
1 teaspoon paprika
1 teaspoon ground ginger
1 teaspoon ground mace
2 tablespoons soy sauce
1 tablespoon dry sherry or whisky

FOR THE SKEWERS:
4 plump boneless chicken breasts, skinned
1 medium pineapple

PREPARATION TIME: 45 minutes, plus marinating
COOKING TIME: 6 minutes per batch

1 Using a balloon whisk and a 2.25 litre (4 pint) glass or china bowl, mix all the ingredients for the marinade together to a smooth paste.

2 Cut each breast into approximately 16 even-sized pieces, making 64 chunks in all. Put into the marinade, cover with cling film and leave for 2–3 hours.

3 To peel the pineapple, use a sharp knife and cut off the plume and stalk about 2 cm ($\frac{3}{4}$ inch) down. Cut the skin off, starting at the top and cutting down and under. Cut the fruit into 4 lengthways, then each piece in half again, lengthways. Cut away the core. Cut each strip into approximately 8 pieces, i.e. 64 bits in all.

4 Remove the chicken from the marinade, reserving the marinade. Using 20 bamboo skewers, thread alternate pieces of chicken and pineapple on to the end third of each stick, leaving about 10 cm (4 inches) protruding, which means about 3 pieces of chicken and 3 pieces of pineapple per stick.

5 Preheat the grill to super hot, then grill the skewers 8 cm (3 inches) away from the heat source for 5–6 minutes, turning regularly. Brush with any spare marinade as you go along. They can be kept warm in the oven at 120°C, 250°F, Gas Mark $\frac{1}{2}$.

BABY RAREBITS

MAKES ABOUT 20 PIECES

5 slices white bread
50–75 g (2–3 oz) butter for frying

TOPPING:
1 small onion, finely chopped
$\frac{1}{2}$ × can pale ale
100 g (4 oz) full fat soft cheese
$\frac{1}{4}$ teaspoon mace
2–3 dashes Tabasco sauce
1 whole egg, beaten
1 tablespoon freshly grated Parmesan cheese
20 anchovy fillets, cut in half lengthways
20 fat capers

PREPARATION TIME: 40 minutes
COOKING TIME: 2–3 minutes

1 With a 2.5–4 cm (1–1$\frac{1}{2}$ inch) plain or fluted cutter, cut out about 20 bread croûtons. Heat half the butter in a heavy-bottomed frying pan without browning. Fry the croûtons in 2 batches, on both sides, until golden-brown,

CLOCKWISE FROM THE TOP: Hot roast loin of pork on herb bread; Baby rarebits; Skewers of spiced chicken and pineapple

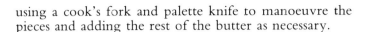

using a cook's fork and palette knife to manoeuvre the pieces and adding the rest of the butter as necessary.

2 Drain on crumpled paper towels, cool, then store in an airtight container, or freeze. [F]

3 Put the onion and beer in a small pan and bring to the boil. Boil rapidly to reduce to 1 tablespoon. Cool.

4 Beat the soft cheese in a bowl with the mace and Tabasco, then beat in the egg mixture and add the strained beer. Beat together well.

5 Spread the mixture evenly on top of each croûton, making a slight mound in the centre. Dredge with a little Parmesan cheese.

6 Put a cross of anchovy fillets over each and press a caper in the top. Preheat the grill to moderate and brown the rarebits until golden and bubbling.

7 Serve hot or warm on a napkin-lined tray or platter.

[F] Freeze for up to 1 month. Thaw for 1 hour at room temperature.

HOT ROAST LOIN OF PORK ON HERB BREAD

SERVES 40

1 × 1.25–1.5 kg (2½–3 lb) loin of pork, boned and rolled

BUTTER:
50 g (2 oz) butter, softened
2 teaspoons French mustard
2 teaspoons dark muscovado sugar
2 teaspoons paprika
2 teaspoons freshly ground black pepper
2 garlic cloves, crushed
1 teaspoon salt

HERB BREAD:
225 g (8 oz) self-raising flour
1 heaped teaspoon salt
1 teaspoon mustard powder
1 tablespoon finely chopped fresh chives and sage
1 tablespoon chopped fresh parsley
75 g (3 oz) dry Cheddar cheese, grated
40 g (1½ oz) butter
2 eggs, beaten
150 ml (¼ pint) milk
apple sauce, to serve
fresh herbs, to garnish

PREPARATION TIME: 35 minutes
COOKING TIME: 1½–1¾ hours
OVEN: 200°C, 400°F, Gas Mark 6, for pork;
190°C, 375°F, Gas Mark 5, for bread

1 Ask your butcher to take the crackling off the pork. Score the top 5 mm (¼ inch) deep and at 5 mm (¼ inch) intervals diagonally both ways across the top of the fat.

2 Using a palette knife, make a paste of all the butter ingredients on a plate, then dab over the pork and spread well in.

3 Roast in a preheated oven for 45 minutes–1 hour.

4 Meanwhile, make the bread. Butter a 450 g (1 lb) loaf tin. Mix all the dry ingredients together, including the cheese.

5 Melt the butter and add to the dry ingredients, together with the beaten egg. Stir to mix well.

6 Place in the prepared tin and bake in a preheated oven for 35–40 minutes. Allow to cool in the tin.

7 Slice the pork and cut into thin strips. Cut the herb bread into thin slices and then cut in half. Spread each half with a little apple sauce and arrange some pork strips on top. Garnish and serve.

Dinner

Dinnertime is so frequently seen as the only time to entertain others, that the idea of laying the dinner table just for you and your spouse, or the family, is overlooked as one of the pleasantest forms of entertainment. An elegant dinner, quietly paced and deliciously cooked, along with a calming quaff from a bottle of wine to soothe those tattered nerves, even the enjoyment of seeing your favourite china, glass and silver being used, just for the family, can be a luxurious and therapeutic treat.
Of course we will also carry on using the evening as the best, if not only time, to push the boat out, give of our best, and greet our friends at our own tables. It is for both these occasions that I have created the following menus.

A Candlelit Dinner for Two

SMOKED SALMON AND SHRIMP TARTARE

SPICED GRILLED CHICKEN WITH WARM VEGETABLE VINAIGRETTE

APPLE AND ROSE PETAL CREAM ICE

I have devised this menu so that you can entertain the special person in your life with the minimum of disruption once all is prepared.

To set the scene, candlelight is the most flattering of lighting as long as there is enough of it. Two candles on the dinner table just won't do. Two on the coffee table, yes, but there must be pools of soft light elsewhere in the room, from dimmed uplighter, picture lights or other groups of candles.

Place the candles on the table so that conversation is easy and your guest's face is flattered by the flames. Low candle holders give a more flattering light than tall sticks.

A guest must not be left alone for more than mere seconds; those few seconds it takes to bring the main course to the table. Everything else should be elegantly arranged on a sideboard, or, better still, on a small table, attractively draped and placed within hands' reach.

The delicious and exotic starter with its dry toast or crackers is there, covered, and ready to be slipped into place when the moment to start is imminent. The chicken dish is already attractively arranged and being kept warm. The cooling, scented ice cream is ready in a wide-mouthed thermos container and finally, an excellent high-roast coffee is also in the room, together with coffee cups, sugar and cream. Brandy and fresh cream chocolates are extra-indulgent additions.

TOP: Spiced grilled chicken with warm vegetable vinaigrette
BOTTOM: Smoked salmon and shrimp tartare

SMOKED SALMON AND SHRIMP TARTARE

SERVES 2

100–150 g (4–5 oz) Scotch smoked salmon
75–100 g (3–4 oz) freshly peeled prawns or shrimps
2 anchovy fillets, finely chopped

DRESSING:
1 tablespoon capers, well drained
½ tablespoon very finely chopped onion (optional)
1 egg yolk
1 teaspoon French mustard
2 tablespoons good olive oil
juice of ½ lemon
freshly ground black pepper

GARNISH:
2 quails' eggs or ½ hen's egg, hard-boiled
capers
whole prawns or shrimps (optional)
50 g (2 oz) salmon caviar or red lumpfish roe (optional)
fingers of dry brown toast, to serve

PREPARATION TIME: 30 minutes

1 Mince, or very finely chop, the smoked salmon, prawns or shrimps and anchovy (a blender or food processor gives the wrong texture) and put into a basin.

2 Mix all the dressing ingredients together, adding salt if needed (smoked salmon and anchovy tend to be salty).

3 Mix the 2 components well together, then divide into 2 portions and press each into a round 'cake' shape with a fork. Garnish with quails' eggs, extra capers and the odd shrimp or prawn if liked. For an even more luxurious starter, spoon 25 g (1 oz) of salmon caviar or even red lumpfish roe on top of each tartare. Serve with toast.

SPICED GRILLED CHICKEN

SERVES 2

2 × 175 g (6 oz) boned chicken breasts, skinned

MARINADE:
1 small garlic clove, crushed
1 teaspoon salt
1 teaspoon freshly ground black pepper
1 teaspoon ground mace
1 teaspoon ground ginger
1 tablespoon rich olive (or soy) oil
1 tablespoon soy sauce
1 tablespoon Amontillado sherry
2–3 dashes Tabasco sauce

PREPARATION TIME: 10 minutes, plus marinating overnight
COOKING TIME: 10 minutes

1 Make *shallow* incisions diagonally both ways across the flesh of the chicken breasts, at 8 mm (⅓ inch) intervals.

2 Place all the ingredients for the marinade in a screw-top jar and shake together well.

3 Put the breasts in a shallow dish. Pour over the marinade, cover and leave for 4–6 hours or overnight.

4 Preheat the grill to searing hot. Brush the hot grill pan with oil. Grill the chicken breasts 10 cm (4 inches) away from the heat source for 4–5 minutes on each side, turning 2–3 times and basting with any surplus marinade. Keep warm whilst you eat your first course.

WARM VEGETABLE VINAIGRETTE

SERVES 2

1 small cauliflower, broken into small florets
2 good 'knobs' of broccoli, broken into small florets

DRESSING:
juice of ½ lemon
25 g (1 oz) good butter
½ teaspoon grated lemon rind
freshly ground black pepper
a dredge of ground mace

PREPARATION TIME: 10 minutes, plus cooling
COOKING TIME: 10 minutes

1 In a large pan of salted boiling water blanch the cauliflower for 2–3 minutes and the broccoli for 1½ to 2 minutes. They should both remain somewhat crisp.

2 Drain, then rinse under cold running water for 10 minutes. When cold, drain, shake dry and store in a plastic-lidded container until ready for use.

3 Heat the dressing ingredients together in a large pan, without browning.

4 Transfer the 2 vegetables to a wire basket, which will fit inside a second large pan of boiling salted water. As you sit down to dinner, put this second pan to boil.

5 When you're ready, immerse the vegetables in the sieve in the boiling water for 1½ minutes. Drain, shaking well, and tip the florets into the hot dressing. Toss over a low heat until hot (half-a-minute). Spoon on to warm dinner plates and arrange the chicken pieces on top.

APPLE AND ROSE PETAL CREAM ICE

SERVES 12

450 ml ($\frac{3}{4}$ pint) stock syrup (opposite)
450 ml ($\frac{3}{4}$ pint) concentrated apple juice
half egg white, beaten lightly
3 teaspoons rose-flower water
3 drops only red food colouring
200 ml ($\frac{1}{3}$ pint) double cream, whipped to soft peak
crystallized rose petals, to decorate

PREPARATION TIME: 5 minutes, plus freezing

It is always useful to have a home-made ice cream or water ice to hand, so make enough for 12 people. Thin ice cream is as fresh and delicate as an English garden.

1 Put all the ingredients, except the cream, into an ice cream churn. When the ice is ribboning and looks a delicate creamy pink, spoon in the cream and freeze until slushy. If you do not have a churn, mix together all the ingredients except the cream and put into a freezer container; freeze until slushy (about 2–3 hours), taking out of the freezer to stir occasionally. Add the cream, beat with a balloon whisk and freeze again. Beat the mixture twice more at hourly intervals. A

2 Scoop out the ice cream using the larger bowl of a melon baller, dipping it into warm water between each scoop. Serve in a frosted wine glass, topped with a crystallized rose petal or two. To frost the edge of each glass, dip the rim into a little frothy egg white, then into granulated sugar. Chill the glasses.

A Crystals will form if the ice cream is kept too cold.

STOCK SYRUP FOR WATER ICES

Glucose syrup is available from dispensing chemists and some grocers.

750 g (1$\frac{1}{2}$ lb) caster sugar
900 ml (1$\frac{1}{2}$ pints) water
100 ml (3$\frac{1}{2}$ fl oz) glucose syrup

COOKING TIME: 2–3 minutes

1 Place all the ingredients together in a meticulously clean pan and bring to the boil. Bubble for 2–3 minutes, when the syrup will be quite clear.

2 Cool, then strain through a conical sieve to rid the syrup of any scum. Store in a screw-topped jar in the refrigerator. The syrup will keep for some weeks.

Spring Dinner Party for Six

CHILLED FENNEL AND APPLE SOUP

ROAST BONED LOIN OF LAMB WITH ROSEMARY AND LEEK SAUCE

SPINACH WITH LEMON, NUTMEG AND GARLIC

NEW POTATOES WITH NUTMEG

PEARS IN SAUTERNE WITH CANDIED LEMON SPIRALS

Many people do enjoy celebrating the seasons, although now that the commercial scene has made foods available all year round, we tend to have strawberries at Christmas and turkey no matter what the month.

However, when entertaining in springtime, I'm sure most of us still think of lamb, whether it is Welsh, Scottish or Southdown. We think also of young, green vegetables and the first new potatoes. Match these in your place settings with a yellow, white and green scheme, the time-honoured spring colours, and produce a delightful dinner party to coincide with that first breath of spring.

CHILLED FENNEL AND APPLE SOUP

SERVES 5–6

2 tablespoons soy or olive oil
1 × 100 g (4 oz) onion, finely chopped
1 head fennel, about 275–350 g (10–12 oz) in weight, trimmed, and cut into 2.5 cm (1 inch) dice
225 g (8 oz) potatoes, peeled and cubed
1 garlic clove, crushed
1 small bay leaf or $\frac{1}{2}$ larger one
1 teaspoon fennel seeds or celery seeds, loosely tied in a piece of muslin
salt
freshly ground black pepper
2–3 teaspoons lemon juice
600 ml (1 pint) Rich Chicken Stock (page 22) or 1 stock cube with 600 ml (1 pint) water
300 ml ($\frac{1}{2}$ pint) unsweetened apple juice

GARNISH (optional):
300 ml ($\frac{1}{4}$ pint) single cream or
200 ml ($\frac{1}{3}$ pint) plain unsweetened yogurt, chilled
2 tablespoons chopped fresh fennel fronds
2 Cox's apples, peeled, cored, finely diced and bathed in lemon juice to prevent discoloration

PREPARATION TIME: 45 minutes, plus chilling overnight
COOKING TIME: 35–40 minutes

1 Warm the oil in a large pan. Add the onion, cover and soften over a low heat for about 8–10 minutes without allowing it to colour. Add the fennel and potatoes and continue cooking in the same manner for a further 10 minutes, stirring from time to time.

2 Add all the seasoning, the stock and the apple juice. Bring to the boil and simmer until the potatoes 'fall', about 15 minutes.

3 Strain into a clean bowl through a wide fine mesh strainer, reserving the vegetable pulp. Leave to cool, when surplus oils will rise to the surface of the liquid. Skim these off and discard.

4 Make a fine purée of the vegetable pulp using a blender or food processor. Stir the purée into the cooled, skimmed liquid. Cover with cling film and chill overnight or for 4–6 hours. Ⓐ

5 When ready to serve, whisk in the chilled cream or yogurt. Sprinkle each serving with a little chopped fennel and add a teaspoonful of diced apple. *Pictured overleaf.*

Ⓐ The soup can be made up to 2 days in advance.

ROAST BONED LOIN OF LAMB WITH ROSEMARY AND LEEK SAUCE

SERVES 6

2 single sprigs fresh rosemary or lavender (see below)
1 × 1¾–2¼ kg (4–5 lb) loin of lamb, boned, skinned, rolled and tied
75 g (3 oz) butter, softened
1 teaspoon salt
1 teaspoon dried thyme
1 teaspoon ground rosemary
1 teaspoon freshly ground black pepper

PREPARATION TIME: 15 minutes
COOKING TIME: 45 minutes–1 hour
OVEN: 240°C, 475°F, Gas Mark 9;
then: 200°C, 400°F, Gas Mark 6

Take the sprigs along to your butcher and ask him to tie the herbs inside the lamb before he rolls and ties it.

1 Make shallow incisions diagonally across the fat of the lamb, both ways. Call it deep scoring if you like.

2 Make a paste of all the other ingredients, then spread and rub this into the fat. Ⓐ

3 Stand the loin on a rack. Place in a preheated oven and roast for 20 minutes, then reduce the heat and continue roasting for a further 25–30 minutes, or longer if you like lamb well done.

4 Leave to stand for 20 minutes before carving in 5 mm (¼ inch) thick slices. Serve with the leek sauce.

Ⓐ Can be prepared the day before and refrigerated.

LEEK SAUCE

25 g (1 oz) unsalted butter
225 g (8 oz) young green leeks, shredded, washed and drained
1 garlic clove, crushed
65 ml (2½ fl oz) single cream
3 teaspoons lemon juice
salt
about 65 ml (2½ fl oz) chicken stock or cold water

PREPARATION TIME: 10 minutes
COOKING TIME: 20–25 minutes

1 Melt the butter in a medium pan over a low heat, without colouring.

2 Add the leeks and garlic, cover and soften them over a low heat stirring or tossing the pan at regular intervals.

3 Pass the leeks and their juices through a blender, then rub through a fine meshed sieve for a really smooth sauce. This is optional but preferable! Ⓐ

4 Return the sauce to the rinsed-out pan and stir in the cream and lemon juice. Season lightly with salt only. Reheat, adding enough stock or water to arrive at a rich pouring consistency.

Ⓐ Can be prepared up to a day in advance, then kept chilled and covered.

SPINACH WITH LEMON, NUTMEG AND GARLIC

SERVES 4–6

1 kg (2 lb) fresh spinach, washed, trimmed of stalks
75 g (3 oz) unsalted butter
1 garlic clove, crushed
salt
freshly ground black pepper
1 teaspoon ground nutmeg
1 tablespoon lemon juice

PREPARATION TIME: 10 minutes
COOKING TIME: 5 minutes

Nutmeg is used with both vegetables because it is often better to match and complement flavours than to contrast them deliberately. Try it – you'll soon see what I mean.

1 Pat the spinach dry. Melt the butter with the garlic in a large deep pan, without colouring it, then add the spinach. Cover, then, over a medium heat, let the spinach 'sink' and wilt, about 3–4 minutes. You will need to fork it around in the early stages.

2 As soon as it is hot, season with salt, pepper, nutmeg and lemon juice, mixing it well in. Do not drain.

NEW POTATOES WITH NUTMEG

SERVES 6

1 kg (2 lb) new potatoes, about 3 cm (1½ inches) in diameter, washed and scraped
25 g (1 oz) butter
½ teaspoon grated nutmeg

PREPARATION TIME: 15 minutes
COOKING TIME: 20 minutes

Allow 5–6 potatoes per person.

1 Boil the potatoes in the usual way, then drain well.

2 Melt the butter in the rinsed-out pan without colouring. Return the potatoes to the pan and toss in the butter, whilst dredging them with the nutmeg. Transfer to a warm lidded tureen. Ⓐ

Ⓐ The potatoes can be cooked half-an-hour before dinner and kept in a hot plate or oven 110°C, 225°F, Gas Mark ¼.

PEARS IN SAUTERNE WITH CANDIED LEMON SPIRALS

SERVES 6

3 lemons
6 large ripe Comice pears
100 g (4 oz) caster sugar
450 ml (¾ pint) Sauterne or other sweet white wine

PREPARATION TIME: 30 minutes
COOKING TIME: 5–30 minutes

The cooking time varies greatly: ripe soft pears will take 5–6 minutes, hard pears can take 20–30 minutes.

1 Using a cannelle knife cut one long spiral of lemon peel from each lemon: start at the top of the lemon and work round and round in one long cut to the other end. Put the rind aside and squeeze the juice into a basin.

2 Cut into the 'flower' end of the pears with a potato peeler, removing about 2 cm (1 inch) from the bottom of the core, then peel the pears, leaving the stalks intact.

3 With a cannelle knife, cut 4–6 spiral channels up the side of the pear flesh starting at the base and curving to the top. The channels should be 2 cm (¾ inch) apart at the base end. Bathe the pears in the lemon juice.

4 In an enamel or stainless steel pan large enough to fit the pears on their sides, add the remaining lemon juice, the sugar, the wine and the spirals of lemon rind to the pan and bring to the boil. Simmer the pears in the mixture until they appear translucent and are cooked (turn them at 5-minutes intervals using 2 tablespoons).

5 Remove the pears to a serving dish and chill. Continue boiling the wine syrup until it is almost as thick as warm golden syrup. Leave it to cool, then chill.

6 Remove the spirals of lemon rind, cut and press them into the cuts in the pears. Trim off any excess peel. Spoon a little of the syrup over each pear and serve. Any remaining syrup can be refrigerated in an airtight container.

CLOCKWISE FROM THE TOP: Pears in Sauterne; Roast boned loin of lamb with rosemary and leek sauce; Spinach with lemon, nutmeg and garlic; New potatoes with nutmeg; Chilled fennel and apple soup

A Summer Dinner for Eight in the Garden

CHILLED CRAB SALAD

WHOLEMEAL BREAD WITH CHIVE BUTTER

TERRINE OF DUCKLING WITH FOIE DE CANARD
AND PISTACHIO NUTS

PINEAPPLE AND ENDIVE SALAD WITH WALNUTS

CHILLED REDCURRANT SOUFFLÉ

ICED COFFEE WITH BRANDY AND CREAM

*W*hilst we do have the perfect climate in Britain for dining out of doors, sadly we don't have perfect weather to go with it! I take the optimistic attitude of *aiming* to eat outside. If it rains? Move in!

As an apéritif I suggest a cooling 'spritzer' made with sparkling water and a bottle of the aromatic Vin de Pêche – an elegant drink, whose delicate flavour is provided by marinating peach kernels in white wine for years. I serve this over crushed ice, in tall glasses with a split strawberry slipped over the rim or a slice of fresh peach in the ice.

I like to offer a simple tray of hot tartlets (see page 110 for example) with pre-dinner drinks – giving that element of the unexpected, for the rest of the meal will most likely be a cold, though balanced, menu of a rich starter, deceptively simple main dish and a frothy pink chilled mousse to close

With the food I find it as interesting to serve two or three different white wines, as it is to show a clutch of different red vintages for an autumn or winter occasion. A full dry white wine from the Rhône would make a good introduction to my dinner and would marry well with the rich crab salad. This could be followed with one of those delicious spicy, almost herby wines from Alsace – a Gewurztraminer. Alternatively, for a total change, why not experiment and serve a dry Tokay. These wines (which come from Alsace as well as Hungary) are almost reminiscent of a light dry sherry and are excellent foils to any main dish where you might otherwise be thinking of serving a fuller-bodied red wine.

I almost always advocate a well-chilled dessert wine at the end of dinner, *but*, poured *before* puddings, cheese, fruit and coffee have already been served. This way they can be sipped at leisure.

CHILLED CRAB SALAD

SERVES 8

225 g (8 oz) cottage cheese, drained if necessary
120 ml (4 fl oz) soured cream, half whipped
1 heaped teaspoon horseradish relish
salt
freshly ground black pepper
1 tablespoon lemon juice
2–3 dashes Tabasco sauce
350 g (12 oz) fresh white crab meat, flaked
175 g (6 oz) celery, finely diced
100 g (4 oz) cucumber, unpeeled but seeded and finely diced
6 spring onions, finely shredded
1 head endive or young lettuce leaves, to serve

GARNISH:
2 tomatoes, skinned, seeded and cut into petals
8 quails' eggs, halved or 2 hard-boiled eggs, quartered
1 spring onion, trimmed and cut lengthways into strips

PREPARATION TIME: 45 minutes

As an added luxury for a summer occasion, serve separately an extra cracked crab claw and a wedge of lemon.

1 Place the cottage cheese, soured cream and horseradish in a bowl and mix well together, seasoning handsomely with salt, pepper and lemon juice to taste. Add some Tabasco sparingly but enough to give the dressing some kick.

2 Combine the crab meat, celery, cucumber and spring onions in a second bowl, then fold them into the cheese and cream mixture. It should not be too sloppy. Chill well.

3 Chill a serving bowl, line it with the endive or lettuce leaves, then spoon in the salad and garnish.

4 Keep chilled, covered with cling film, until ready to eat. Serve with brown bread and chive butter.

CHIVE BUTTER

1 small bunch of chives, finely chopped
175 g (6 oz) butter, softened
2 teaspoons lemon juice
1 teaspoon salt
freshly ground black pepper

1 Mix all the ingredients together and place in a small bowl. Serve with wholemeal bread. Freeze any left over for future use.

TERRINE OF DUCKLING WITH FOIE DE CANARD AND PISTACHIO NUTS

CLOCKWISE FROM THE TOP: Terrine of duckling with pineapple and endive salad (page 108); Iced crab salad; Wholemeal bread with chive butter

SERVES 8

350 g (12 oz) streaky bacon, rinded
1 × 1.75 kg (4 lb) duck, with liver
2 pieces stem ginger, finely chopped
1 teaspoon ground ginger
4 tablespoons demerara rum
175 g (6 oz) pork, lean
175 g (6 oz) pork fat
1 egg
3 teaspoons salt
1 teaspoon freshly ground black pepper
1 teaspoon paprika
75 g (3 oz) pistachio nuts, split or roughly chopped
1 × 150 g (5 oz) tin or 'bloc' Foie de Canard
apple or Cumberland sauce, to serve

PREPARATION TIME: 50 minutes, plus marinating and cooling
COOKING TIME: 1¼ hours
OVEN: 200°C, 400°F, Gas Mark 6

Make 3–4 days in advance rather than freezing. It *is* expensive, so keep for high days.

1 Lightly oil a 25–30 cm (10–12 inch) long iron terrine or seamless loaf tin.

2 With the back of a wetted knife, stretch each rasher of bacon before using to line the mould (this prevents shrinkage of the bacon).

3 Remove the breasts from the duck. Remove the skin from the breasts and discard, then remove the legs and skin them. Cut the meat from the legs and carcass.

4 Put the 2 duck breasts (whole) into a basin with the liver, the 2 gingers and the rum. Marinate for 2 hours.

5 Put the leg meat, pork, fat, egg, salt, pepper, paprika and liquor from the marinade into a food processor or liquidizer and blend to a fine purée. Turn the mixture into a basin, mix in the pistachio nuts and the duck liver, cut into smallish pieces.

6 Put a third of the mixture into the bacon-lined mould, pressing well in with the back of a wetted spoon. Using a hot knife, cut the foie de canard lengthways into 3 thick slices. Lay these end to end in the terrine, trimming to fit.

7 Spread and press over another third of the purée, then lay in the 2 duck breasts, end to end. Cover with a final layer of the mixture, smoothing the top and pressing well into the corners. Cover with a lid or foil.

8 Cook in a bain-marie of boiling water in a preheated oven for 1¼ hours.

9 Cool completely. Press with a piece of foil-covered board and a weight, then refrigerate. Leave to mature for a couple of days.

10 Serve cut in 5 mm (¼ inch) slices – no thicker – with apple or Cumberland sauce. Serve baby buttered new potatoes on a separate plate as a hot accompaniment.

PINEAPPLE AND ENDIVE SALAD WITH WALNUTS

SERVES 8

4 heads Belgian endive, separated and washed
½ a ripe pineapple, knife-peeled and cored or use 1 × 350 g
(12 oz) can pineapple rings
1 bunch watercress, picked and washed

DRESSING:
150 ml (¼ pint) plain unsweetened yogurt
juice of ½ lemon, strained
1 tablespoon Blossom honey (or other mild honey)
1 teaspoon mild French mustard
salt
freshly ground black pepper

50 g (2 oz) walnuts, roughly crushed, to garnish

PREPARATION TIME: 30 minutes

1 Break or cut the endive into even-sized pieces. Cut the pineapple into rings, then into fan-shaped pieces. Break the watercress into small sprigs. Ⓐ

2 Put all the ingredients for the dressing in a screw-top jar and shake together until smooth and creamy. Ⓐ

3 Mix all the salad ingredients together and transfer to a salad bowl.

4 Spoon or dribble over the dressing and sprinkle with the crushed walnuts. *Pictured on page 107.*

Ⓐ The salad ingredients can be prepared the night before; each stored in a sealed bag and kept chilled.
   The dressing can be made 2 days before and kept chilled.

CHILLED REDCURRANT SOUFFLÉ

SERVES 8

450 g (1 lb) redcurrants
50 ml (2 fl oz) water
50 g (2 oz) sugar
6 whole eggs, separated plus 4 yolks
50 g (2 oz) caster sugar
150 ml (¼ pint) lemon juice (3 lemons)
1 sachet gelatine crystals
300 ml (½ pint) double cream, half whipped
1 teaspoon carmine or cochineal colour

GARNISH:
clusters of redcurrants
sprigs of mint

PREPARATION TIME: 20 minutes, plus cooling
COOKING TIME: 8–10 minutes

1 Place the redcurrants, water and sugar in a pan and simmer until the fruit has pulped, about 8–10 minutes. Strain through a fine sieve, pressing the pulp through. You should have 300 ml (½ pint) of purée.

2 Place a large 4.5 litre (8 pint) heatproof glass bowl over a pan of boiling water. Add the yolks, caster sugar, redcurrant purée, lemon juice and the gelatine crystals and beat with a balloon whisk until the whisk leaves a distinct trail.

3 Stand the basin in a sink of cold water and leave to cool but not set, stirring from time to time.

4 Mix the whipped cream well in (reserving a little for decoration), then mix in the colour. Beat the egg whites until stiff. Whisk in one-third of the beaten egg whites, then cut and fold in the rest. Pour into a 2.25 litre (4 pint) glass dish, cover with cling film and chill. Serve decorated with whipped cream, clusters of redcurrants and fine sprigs of mint.

ICED COFFEE WITH BRANDY AND CREAM

SERVES 8

75 g (3 oz) caster or muscavado sugar
about 1.25 litres (2¼ pints) cold water
6 tablespoons medium to high roast ground coffee
50 ml (2 fl oz) brandy or whisky
125 ml (4 fl oz) double cream

PREPARATION TIME: 15 minutes, plus chilling
COOKING TIME: about 5 minutes

1 Bring the sugar and 85 ml (3 fl oz) of the water to boil. Simmer until dissolved. Cool, chill and store in a jar. Ⓐ

2 Make the coffee using 1.2 litres (2 pints) water by your usual method. Cool, chill and store in a meticulously clean airtight glass, china or plastic container. Ⓐ

3 Fill 8 small wine glasses two-thirds full with the chilled coffee. Add half a tot of brandy or whisky. Sweeten to taste with the sugar syrup.

4 Float a little cream over the top of each glass by pouring over the back of a teaspoon held just on the surface of the coffee and touching the sides of the glass.

Ⓐ The sugar syrup will keep indefinitely.

Iced coffee with brandy and cream; Chilled redcurrant soufflé

*An Elegant
Winter Dinner
for Eight*

HOT TARTLETS OF RAINBOW TROUT AND
COTTAGE CHEESE

COQ AU VIN DE BOURGOGNE AU CASSIS

HOT FLAGEOLET, BACON AND RICE SALAD

APPLE, ORANGE AND CINNAMON ROULADE
WITH APPLE CREAM SAUCE

BABY RAREBITS (page 96)

There are times when we all want to invest a lot of time and trouble to produce something out-of-the-ordinary and dinner time is the time to do it. This menu is designed to be both visually and gastronomically special.

I have discussed the subject of pre-prandial drinks elsewhere (page 13–14) and have described the use of flowers and candlelight for scene-setting (page 10). As a final embellishment, choose music which is soft, meandering and instrumental to complement rather than distract from the atmosphere.

HOT TARTLETS OF RAINBOW TROUT AND COTTAGE CHEESE

MAKES 8

GARLIC PASTRY:
75 g (3 oz) butter
100 g (4 oz) plain white flour
1 egg yolk
1 tablespoon lemon juice
1 small garlic clove, crushed
salt
freshly ground black pepper

FILLING:
2 trout, skinned, boned, filleted and flesh cut into $\frac{1}{2}$ cm ($\frac{1}{4}$ inch) dice
4 spring onions, finely chopped
175 g (6 oz) cottage cheese, drained
2 eggs (size 1), beaten
100 ml (4 fl oz) single cream
175 g (6 oz) fresh or frozen shrimps, thawed

PREPARATION TIME: 40 minutes
COOKING TIME: 45–60 minutes
OVEN: 200°C, 400°F, Gas Mark 6;
then: 160°C, 325°F, Gas Mark 3

1 Rub the butter into the flour until sand-like in texture. Mix the egg yolk, lemon juice, garlic and salt and pepper in a cup. Pour this over the butter and flour and mix to a soft dough, then chill.

2 Roll out thinly and line eight 8 cm (3 inch) lightly buttered patty tins. Prick all over and fit a second patty tin, buttered on the outside, into each. Bake in a preheated oven for 15–20 minutes until crisp. Cool, then remove the 'lining' tins. Ease the pastry shell away from the sides but leave in situ.

3 Mix all the filling ingredients together, cover with cling film and chill until ready for use.

4 Fill the pastry shells with the mixture, reduce the temperature and bake for 30–40 minutes or until the mixture is just set.

LEFT TO RIGHT: Hot flageolet, bacon and rice salad (page 112); Hot tartlets of rainbow trout and cottage cheese; Coq au vin de Bourgogne au cassis

COQ AU VIN DE BOURGOGNE AU CASSIS

SERVES 8

2 × 1.5–1.75 kg (3–4 lb) chickens (or 8 fresh chicken joints)
50 g (2 oz) butter
4 tablespoons rich olive oil
175 g (6 oz) salt pork or belly pork, cut into small cubes
24 pickling onions
6 medium carrots, peeled and sliced
2 garlic cloves, crushed
8 shallots, peeled and finely chopped
6 tablespoons brandy
4 tablespoons cassis liqueur
1 bottle full-bodied red Burgundy
½ pint chicken stock
1 fresh bouquet garni (or sachet)
salt and freshly ground black pepper

PREPARATION TIME: 50 minutes
COOKING TIME: about 1½ hours

1 Using poultry shears, cut each chicken into 4–6 serving pieces.

2 Melt the butter and oil in a heavy-bottomed pan. Brown the pork and onions and remove to a plate with a slotted spoon.

3 Add the chicken pieces to the pan and brown well on both sides. Put in the carrots, garlic, shallots, the pork and onions then pour over the warmed brandy and ignite carefully, standing well back!

4 When the flames have subsided, pour over the cassis liqueur, lower the heat, cover and simmer in the juices for 30 minutes. Pour over the wine mixed with the chicken stock, add the bouquet garni, season well with salt and pepper and cook for a further 30 minutes.

5 Lift out the chicken pieces on to a warm serving dish. Reduce the sauce by half by boiling rapidly, then taste and adjust the seasoning if necessary. Serve with butter-fried croûtons and accompany with the flageolet salad and buttered French beans or broccoli spears.

HOT FLAGEOLET, BACON AND RICE SALAD

SERVES 8

450 g (1 lb) prime back bacon, cut into strips
2 × 400 g (14 oz) cans flageolet beans in brine
175 g (6 oz) rice
1.2 litres (2 pints) strong chicken stock (using 3 stock cubes)
100 g (4 oz) onion, finely chopped
25 g (1 oz) butter
1 garlic clove, crushed (optional)

DRESSING:
85 ml (3 fl oz) olive or nut oil (not corn oil)
40 ml (1½ fl oz) lemon juice
1 teaspoon mild French mustard
1 teaspoon sugar

PREPARATION TIME: 20 minutes
COOKING TIME: 30–40 minutes

1 Fry the bacon until well done, drain and put to keep hot (or reheat when ready for use). Rinse the beans under cold water and drain well. Cook the rice in the chicken stock for 16–18 minutes, stirring to prevent sticking. Drain (retaining the liquid for soup for some other time.)

2 Fry the onion in the butter in a large pan until soft and golden, then stir in the garlic, if using.

3 Put the dressing ingredients into a screw-top jar, season generously with salt and pepper and shake until well mixed. Pour the dressing into the pan of onion and garlic and bring to the boil.

4 Add the rice and beans and, using a slotted spoon, stir until hot right through. Mix in the hot bacon, then spoon into a warm serving dish. *Pictured on page 111.*

APPLE, ORANGE AND CINNAMON ROULADE WITH APPLE CREAM SAUCE

SERVES 6–8

ROULADE:
2 large eggs
65 g (2½ oz) caster sugar
2 teaspoons orange peel, grated or shredded
50 g (2 oz) plain flour sieved with 1 teaspoon cinnamon
dredging of caster or icing sugar
275 g (10 oz) rindless or jelly marmalade

SAUCE:
175 g (6 oz) Cox's apples
50 g (2 oz) caster or soft brown sugar
50 ml (2 fl oz) brandy or water
1 stick of cinnamon or 1 teaspoon ground cinnamon
85 ml (3 fl oz) single cream

TO DECORATE:
1 Cox's apple
juice of ¼ lemon
15 g (½ oz) sugar

PREPARATION TIME: 50 minutes
COOKING TIME: about 30 minutes
OVEN: 190°C, 375°F, Gas Mark 5

1 Grease and line a Swiss roll tin 35 × 23 cm (14 × 9 inches) with buttered paper.

2 Whisk the eggs and sugar until they form a heavy trail, when the whisk is drawn through. Mix in the peel, then cut and fold in the flour mixture. Pour into the prepared tin and spread into the corners.

3 Bake in a preheated oven for 10–12 minutes, or until the cake is firm to the touch in the centre.

4 Meanwhile wring out a tea cloth in cold water and spread on a work surface. Lay over a sheet of greaseproof paper dredged evenly with caster or icing sugar over the cloth. Invert the cooked roulade on to this and carefully remove the lining paper.

5 Roll up fairly tightly lengthways (i.e. making a long slim roll) using the paper and the cloth to help you. The paper stays inside as you roll, the damp cloth does not. Leave to cool.

6 Once cool, unroll the roulade and spread with plenty of jelly. Re-roll without the paper and dredge with more caster or icing sugar. F Cut into 6 V-shaped wedges (and eat the offcuts from each end!).

Apple, orange and cinnamon roulade with apple cream sauce

7 To make the sauce, peel and core the apples, slice thinly and toss in the sugar. Add the brandy or water and cinnamon and cook, covered, over a minimum heat until pulped. Remove the cinnamon stick, if used. Place in a liquidizer or food processor and purée. Cool, stir in the cream then chill.

8 To decorate, peel and core the single apple. Cut it into 12 slim wedges and toss in the lemon juice and sugar. Cook together in a shallow pan in one layer over a minimum heat, covered, until transparent but still holding their shape. Leave to cool. F

9 Serve the wedges of roulade decorated with a couple of slivers of cooked apple and a tiny blob of jelly marmalade. It is best eaten the same day, although it can be frozen.

F Freeze the sauce and roulade separately for up to 1 month. Thaw overnight at room temperature.

Pasta Supper Party

COLD

PASTA SHELLS WITH CHICKEN AND SMOKED SALMON

GREEN TAGLIATELLE WITH STRAWBERRIES, PROSCIUTTO AND RED PEPPER CREAM SAUCE

SHRIMP AND SPAGHETTI SALAD

HOT

LINGUINE CON LIMONE

PEPPERONI SALAD

MICHAEL SMITH'S OWN BOLOGNESE SAUCE

*T*here are many occasions when we want to entertain our friends to a casual relaxed evening of chat, wearing nothing more stylish than jeans and jumpers, or to issue a spontaneous invitation after a concert, or some other evening entertainment. Yet the house-keeping cash-flow just isn't flowing, or you are in the middle of an economy drive. At these times, surely everyone turns to the 'cheap-and-cheerful meal' and pasta is the answer for your menu.

It is quick to prepare, tasty, filling and can be as rich or simple in composition as you choose to make it. In addition it can, surprisingly to some, be served hot or cold. Choose from the menu the number of dishes to suit the number of people you are entertaining but include at least one cold dish.

If you are a pasta addict, as I am, or if there is a possibility that pals or family may be descending on you but nothing *concrete* has been arranged, then you'll keep a batch of cooked pasta ready in the refrigerator. This is so easy to do (see page 17) – and if the casual drop-in doesn't materialize, then you just have pasta for lunch or supper the next day.

LEFT TO RIGHT ABOVE: Pasta shells with chicken and smoked salmon; Green tagliatelle with strawberries, prosciutto and red pepper cream sauce

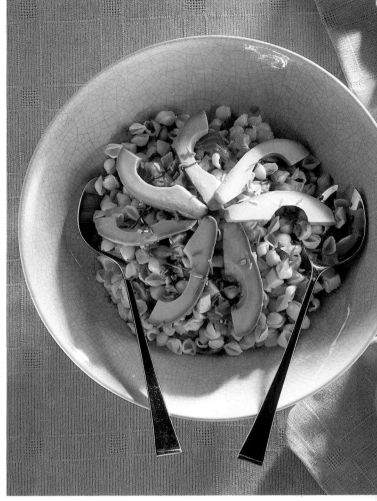

PASTA SHELLS WITH CHICKEN AND SMOKED SALMON

SERVES 6 (or more as a starter or as part of a buffet)

1 × 225 g (8 oz) packed small pasta shells
2 garlic cloves, crushed
1 teaspoon salt
1 teaspoon freshly ground white pepper
1 rounded teaspoon English mustard
150 ml ($\frac{1}{4}$ pint) rich olive oil
juice of 2 lemons
350 g (12 oz) cooked chicken breast, diced
100 g (4 oz) smoked salmon, diced
2 avocados
Tabasco sauce (optional)
1 tablespoon finely chopped fresh parsley and/or chives

PREPARATION TIME: 20 minutes, plus chilling
COOKING TIME: about 10 minutes

I have been serving pasta this way for decades; I have no idea where or when the idea came to me, but it is good, and can't go wrong.

1 Boil the pasta shells in an abundance of water until *al dente*. Rinse under cold running water and drain well, shaking the water out of the cavities.

2 Put the garlic, salt, white pepper, mustard, olive oil and juice of 1 of the lemons into a screw-top jar and shake together until well mixed.

3 Mix the pasta shells with the chicken and salmon in a large bowl, pour over the dressing and toss well. Cover with cling film and leave to chill for 2–3 hours.

4 To prepare the avocados, cut each fruit in half, twist to separate the 2 parts and lift out the stone. Peel the fruits, cut into long slices and mix with the juice of the second lemon immediately to prevent discoloration. Just before you are ready to use them, season the slices lightly with salt and pepper and a dash or two of Tabasco if you like your food hot!

5 Assemble the dish by arranging the slices of avocado in a star shape over the chicken and salmon and pasta, incorporating any juices into the salad. Sprinkle liberally with the chopped parsley and/or chives.

GREEN TAGLIATELLE WITH STRAWBERRIES, PROSCIUTTO AND RED PEPPER CREAM SAUCE

SERVES 5–6 as a starter, or 4 as a main course

4 large ripe red peppers
4 tablespoons olive or soya oil
2 shallots, or 25 g (1 oz) onions, finely chopped
1 large garlic clove, crushed
¼ chicken stock cube
1 heaped teaspoon sweet paprika
¼ teaspoon mild curry powder
2 teaspoons sugar
1 teaspoon salt
½ teaspoon freshly ground black pepper
350 g (12 oz) ripe strawberries, quartered
150 ml (¼ pint) single cream (optional)
750 g (1½ lb) green tagliatelle
50 g (2 oz) unsalted butter
100 g (4 oz) prosciutto, cut into ribbons

PREPARATION TIME: 30 minutes
COOKING TIME: 40–45 minutes

1 To make the sauce, skin 3 of the peppers by spearing each one on a long-tined fork and blistering over a flame (this takes 5–10 minutes). Alternatively, preheat the grill to very hot and grill the peppers until blistered. Peel off the skin under cold running water, then remove seeds and cut away any ribs of pith. Chop roughly and put aside.

2 Heat 2 tablespoons of the oil in a heavy-bottomed pan. Add the shallots and garlic and fry until lightly golden. Dissolve the stock cube in 150 ml (½ pint) water. Add this, plus the paprika, curry powder, sugar, salt, pepper and 6 of the quartered strawberries to the shallots. Add the prepared peppers and stir in well. Lower the heat and cook gently for 15–20 minutes until soft.

3 Transfer the sauce to a liquidizer or food processor and purée. For extra refinement, finish by rubbing through a fine-mesh sieve. Reheat, stirring, and add the cream if used. (This makes it a much richer dish.) [A]

4 Cook the pasta in boiling water to which 2 tablespoons oil have been added, then drain well.

5 Remove the seeds from the remaining pepper and cut into fine julienne strips. Warm the butter without browning in a large non-stick pan, add the julienne of peppers and soften these for a minute or so without browning. Mix in the cooked pasta to coat and reheat. Fork on to a platter. Scatter with the remaining strawberries and prosciutto. Serve the sauce separately.

[A] The sauce can be made 3 days in advance, covered and chilled.

SHRIMP AND SPAGHETTI SALAD

SERVES 4–6

120 ml (4 fl oz) rich olive oil
25 ml (1 fl oz) red wine vinegar
2 large garlic cloves, finely chopped or crushed
salt
plenty of freshly ground black pepper
450 g (1 lb) spaghetti, cooked
450 g (1 lb) peeled prawns or shrimps
1 heaped tablespoon chopped fresh parsley
2 heaped tablespoons snipped chives

PREPARATION TIME: 5 minutes
COOKING TIME: 12–15 minutes (for the spaghetti)

CLOCKWISE FROM THE TOP: Michael Smith's own bolognese sauce;
Shrimp and spaghetti salad; Pepperoni salad; Linguine con limone

I have been eating this simple cold pasta dish almost weekly for over a quarter of a century, so that tells you how good it is. My former wife first introduced it to me before we were married: it had been a great stand-by at their country house in the Haut Savoie in France. You could try using vermicelli instead of the spaghetti for an unusual effect. Fresh or vacuum-packed prawns or shrimps are best. If you use frozen ones, let them thaw gradually overnight in the refrigerator. Do not force them by running hot water over them. Everything can be made a day in advance, tossing the salad together half-an-hour before serving.

1 Put the oil, vinegar, garlic, salt and pepper into a screw-topped jar and shake until well mixed.

2 Put the spaghetti and prawns into a serving bowl. Half-an-hour before serving, sprinkle over the herbs, pour over the dressing and toss well together.

LINGUINE CON LIMONE
(Thin pasta with lemon sauce)

SERVES 4

3.5 litres (6 pints) water
1¼ tablespoons salt
350 g (12 oz) linguine

LEMON SAUCE:
250 ml (8 fl oz) double cream (or thin béchamel sauce)
40 g (1½ oz) butter
finely shredded peel of 2 lemons
salt
freshly ground black pepper

PREPARATION TIME: 10 minutes
COOKING TIME: 12–15 minutes

If you cannot obtain linguine, then use tagliolini, spaghettini or fettucine. In fact, what is being asked for is 'small bore' pasta, which adds to the elegance of this simple but effective dish.

1 Bring the water to the boil and add the salt. Lower the pasta in all at the same time, so that it cooks evenly, 'blending' it into a rapid boil, stirring with a wooden spoon or wooden pasta fork to separate the strands. Cook until it is *al dente*, about 8–10 minutes.

2 Meanwhile, make the sauce. Heat the cream, butter and lemon peel in another pan large enough to contain the cooked pasta. Season well with salt and pepper.

3 As soon as the pasta is *al dente*, drain well, toss in the hot cream, using 2 forks until all the strands are coated with the sauce. Serve straight away.

PEPPERONI SALAD

SERVES 6–8

1 kg (2 lb) green, red and/or yellow peppers, washed
300 ml (½ pint) rich olive oil
2 garlic cloves, cut in half
salt
freshly ground black pepper

GARNISH:
2 large sprigs of fresh parsley or basil, finely chopped
anchovy fillets (optional)

PREPARATION TIME: 15 minutes, plus chilling
COOKING TIME: 20 minutes

Further proof that I now love cooked peppers come with this traditional Italian recipe. Ideal with pasta.

1 Cut the peppers in half, remove the seeds and cut out all the core and pith. Cut them into long strips, 8 mm (⅓ inch) wide.

2 Heat the oil in a frying pan. Fry the garlic gently until it browns remove with a slotted spoon and discard.

3 Add the strips of pepper, cover and cook them very gently for 15 minutes. Season with salt and pepper, cool, then chill.

4 Garnish with parsley or basil and a few anchovy fillets if liked.

MICHAEL SMITH'S OWN BOLOGNESE SAUCE

MAKES 1.2 litres (2 pints), SERVES 10–12

350 g (12 oz) best stewing or rump steak
50 g (2 oz) onion, finely chopped
3 tablespoons olive oil
75 g (3 oz) tomato purée
25 g (1 oz) flour
300 ml (½ pint) red wine
1 large garlic clove, crushed
300 ml (½ pint) stock (use a stock cube)
salt
freshly ground black pepper

PREPARATION TIME: 15 minutes
COOKING TIME: about 1 hour

The Italian Bolognese Sauce is somewhat lighter than my version. I make a richer sauce by using all wine instead of half stock half wine and I always use rump steak. Fat-free mince is also good.

1 Strip the steak of fat and sinew, then put through a mincer twice or mince in a food processor.

2 Fry the onion in the oil in a heavy-bottomed pan until golden brown. Gradually add the minced meat, stirring well over a good heat until the meat browns. Now reduce the heat and add the tomato purée, taking care to work it well in and see that it does not burn. Sprinkle the flour over and mix well in.

3 Now – and here is the secret of a good brown sauce – over a low heat gradually allow a crust to form on the bottom of the pan. This should take about 10 minutes, but watch it carefully. Remove the mixture to a large dinner plate. Turn up the heat again and pour in the red wine. Using a wooden spatula, work all this crust into a sauce. When the bottom of the pan is clear, put the meat back into the winy sauce, add the garlic and the stock and simmer for 30 minutes. Season lightly. Serve with pasta.

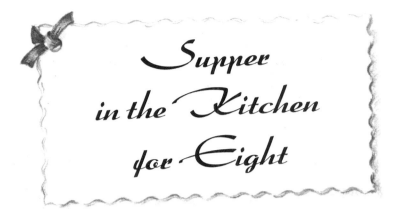

Supper in the Kitchen for Eight

ROOT VEGETABLE SOUP

BOSTON BAKED BEANS

LAMB KOFTAS IN TOMATO SAUCE

SHARP GREEN BEAN SALAD WITH MINT

ETON MESS

*T*here are no hard and fast rules for this most informal way of entertaining, except that guests will be helping themselves from those attractive oven-to-table pans and casseroles straight from cooker top or oven.

Provide a wicker basket of freshly cut chunks of moist wholemeal bread and a slab of chilled butter, set in an attractive earthenware dish of crushed ice – an element of great effect done deliberately to show that your relaxed supper, casual though it may be, has had careful thought given to it.

Bright napkins stuffed into a vase and a trug of dried flowers or autumn-coloured gourds, together with the decorative straw of Chianti fiascos and a group of 5 or 6 different coloured candles in an assortment of holders are all that you need to get the party going.

It is an ideal way of feeding good friends or just the family (what a nice surprise it would make for them!) when you have all been out to an evening entertainment. Finish with some Irish coffee. Pour a tot of Irish whiskey into the coffee and float pouring cream into the cup over the top of an upturned teaspoon, touching the side of the cup.

ROOT VEGETABLE SOUP

SERVES 8–12

450 g (1 lb) each of: potatoes; carrots; swede; parsnips; onions; celeriac; all peeled and roughly diced
2 large garlic cloves, skinned, crushed
2.25 litres (4 pints) water
2 teaspoons salt
100 g (4 oz) butter, to enrich the soup (optional)

BOUQUET:
2 bay leaves
1 sprig thyme or 1 teaspoon dried
1 sprig marjoram or 1 teaspoon dried
1 sprig oregano or 1 teaspoon dried
2 teaspoons peppercorns
1 teaspoon celery seeds

OPTIONAL GARNISHES:
225 g (8 oz) butter-fried baby croûtons and 1 bunch spring onions, trimmed and finely shredded
or
2 bunches chives finely snipped and 2 tablespoons chopped fresh parsley
or
150 ml ($\frac{1}{4}$ pint) double cream

ABOVE: Root vegetable soup; Boston baked beans

PREPARATION TIME: 45 minutes
COOKING TIME: 35–40 minutes

In our efforts to use every conceivable new vegetable on the market, we are tending to forget the wholesome full flavours of our own excellent produce.

Try this basic pure-toned, slightly herby vegetable soup, if only to remind yourself not to miss out on the worthiness of the 'golden-oldies'. The soup relies totally on its own natural flavours: not even chicken stock interferes.

1 Put all the diced vegetables and garlic into a 7 litre (12 pint) pan. Cover with the water and add the salt and the butter, if using. Tie the herbs, peppercorns and celery seeds loosely in muslin and add the bouquet to the pan. Bring to the boil, lower the heat and simmer until all is tender, about 40 minutes. Leave to cool slightly before transferring to a liquidizer or food processor. Blend the mixture to a tweedy texture. Ⓐ Ⓕ

2 Reheat and serve with one (or all!) of the suggested garnishes. The soup can be thinned if necessary with water, stock, single cream or tomato juice.

Ⓐ The soup can be made 1–2 days in advance, covered with cling film and kept chilled.
Ⓕ Freeze for up to 3 months. Reheat gently from frozen, adding 1–2 tablespoons of water at first to prevent sticking.

BOSTON BAKED BEANS

SERVES 6–8

450 g (1 lb) dried white beans
1.2 litre (2 pints) strong ale
450 ml ($\frac{3}{4}$ pint) beef stock
1 tablespoon tomato purée
2 small bay leaves
225 g (8 oz) onion, finely chopped
1 × 5 cm (2 inch) piece green ginger peeled, finely chopped or
1 teaspoon ground ginger
grated zest and juice of 1 lemon
1 tablespoon maple syrup (or corn syrup)
2 tablespoons molasses (or half black treacle, half golden syrup)
2 rounded tablespoons Yorkshire relish or Worcestershire sauce
350 g (12 oz) salted pork, skinned, cut into 5 mm ($\frac{1}{2}$ inch) dice or minced
1 tablespoon mild French mustard
1 teaspoon freshly ground black pepper

TO FINISH:
1 × 1 kg (450 g) joint gammon ham or boiling bacon, soaked overnight in cold water
$\frac{1}{2}$ tablespoon oil

PREPARATION TIME: 30 minutes, plus soaking overnight
COOKING TIME: 6–6$\frac{1}{2}$ hours
OVEN: 185°C, 360°F, Gas Mark 4$\frac{1}{2}$;
then: 180°C, 350°F, Gas Mark 4

1 Soak the beans overnight in 600 ml (1 pint) of the beer (the beans should be covered).

2 Put the soaked beans and their liquid into a 4.5 litre (8 pint) oven-to-table casserole. Add the remaining beer and all the remaining ingredients except the ham or bacon and oil. Cover and cook in the preheated oven for 3 hours. Stir from time to time and as the liquid evaporates add enough water to keep the beans well covered at all times. Do this every half-hour or so.

3 Cut the ham or bacon into 2.5 cm (1 inch) pieces. Heat the oil in a large, heavy-bottomed frying pan until lightly smoking. Put in the pieces of meat and brown over a high heat until nicely coloured on all sides.

4 Transfer the meat to the casserole and mix in with the beans. Reduce the temperature, return the casserole to the oven and continue cooking for a further 3–3$\frac{1}{2}$ hours, this time adding only enough water just to keep the surface of the beans covered. Cook until the meat becomes completely tender and the sauce and beans are a cohered mass. Ⓐ

Ⓐ Many people consider the beans are better when reheated, so the dish can be prepared 2–3 days in advance.

LAMB KOFTAS IN TOMATO SAUCE

SERVES 6–8

750 g (1½ lb) lamb fillet, finely minced
1 × 100 g (4 oz) onion, finely chopped
1 bunch of spring onions, trimmed and finely shredded
2 tablespoons finely chopped fresh parsley
75 g (3 oz) raisins
1 garlic clove, crushed
2 teaspoons ground coriander
1 teaspoon sweet paprika
1 teaspoon finely chopped green ginger
3 teaspoons salt, or less
2 teaspoons finely ground black pepper
2 eggs, beaten

COATING:
a little flour
a little soya or nut oil for frying

TOMATO SAUCE:
1 × 350 g (12 oz) can plum tomatoes
150 ml (¼ pint) tomato juice
1 teaspoon muscovado sugar
¼ teaspoon ground thyme
¼ teaspoon ground bay leaf
3–4 dashes of Tabasco sauce
1 teaspoon mild, sweet paprika
18–20 cherry tomatoes or 5–6 larger tomatoes, quartered

GARNISH:
a little chopped fresh parsley (optional)

PREPARATION TIME: 1¼ hours
COOKING TIME: 50–55 minutes
OVEN: 200°C, 400°F, Gas Mark 6

1 Mix the first 11 ingredients together and bind with the beaten egg. With wetted hands, divide the mixture into 16–20 even-sized pieces, then form them into meatballs between the still wet palms of the hands.

2 Roll in flour, to coat thoroughly.

3 Heat 5 mm (¼ inch) of oil in a large heavy-bottomed frying pan until smoking. Fry the meatballs in 2 batches and brown on all sides. Transfer to a baking dish.

4 To make the sauce; press the plum tomatoes through a fine sieve. Mix with all the remaining ingredients, except the cherry tomatoes. Pour the sauce *around* the meatballs. Disperse the cherry or quartered tomatoes evenly between the koftas. Bake in a preheated oven for 40–45 minutes.

5 Sprinkle with extra parsley, if liked, to garnish.

SHARP GREEN BEAN SALAD WITH MINT

SERVES 8

750 g (1½ lb) green beans, e.g. stick, French, kidney or Kenya, topped, tailed and stringed

DRESSING:
1 large garlic clove, crushed
1 heaped teaspoon mild French mustard
juice of ½ lemon
300 ml (½ pint) plain unsweetened yogurt
salt
freshly ground white pepper
2 tablespoons freshly chopped mint, to garnish

PREPARATION TIME: 10 minutes
COOKING TIME: 2 minutes

1 Drop the whole beans into a large pan of boiling, salted water. Cook for 2 minutes. Drain and cool under running cold water to retain their bright green colour. Drain again.

2 Place in a bowl, cover with cling film and chill.

3 In a basin, mix the garlic, mustard and lemon juice to a paste. Mix in the yogurt and season sparingly with salt and pepper. Toss and coat the beans just before serving.

4 Just before ready to serve, add the beans to the yogurt mixture, tossing to coat well, then sprinkle the chopped mint over this mixture.

ETON MESS

SERVES 8

350 g (12 oz) frozen raspberries
40–50 g (1½–2 oz) caster sugar
juice of ½ lemon, strained
2 tablespoons Kirsch, Drambuie or whisky
600 ml (1 pint) cream, whipped to soft peak
12 meringue shells, roughly crushed
1 kg (2 lb) strawberries, quartered

PREPARATION TIME: 15 minutes
COOKING TIME: 5 minutes

People love doing this for themselves, as did the boys in the 'dorms' of Eton College. I add the luxury of raspberry sauce and liqueur to my game! So, have all the ingredients ready in bowls lined up for people to mix and match as they please.

1 Place the raspberries, sugar and lemon in a small pan over medium heat, cover and cook until soft, stirring regularly.

2 Rub the mixture through a fine sieve. Cool, then cover with cling film and chill.

3 Mix the liqueur with the cream and chill.

CLOCKWISE FROM THE TOP: Lamb koftas in tomato sauce; Eton mess; Sharp green bean salad with mint

4 Place the meringues, strawberries, flavoured cream and raspberry sauce in separate bowls and leave people to help themselves.

Special Occasions

More and more people are entertaining at home these days,
not least because it is expensive to do so in restaurants and
banqueting rooms, or to hire caterers to arrange the affair
in some hall or other. With the exception of business
entertaining, all parties are better for being held against the
backdrop of your own home, reflecting your personality
and where you are most at ease. This chapter is
particularly for when you venture into things on a
somewhat grander scale, as well as including my particular
traditional British favourites.

There is only one reason for giving a party, and that is to
enjoy entertaining your friends, so arrange the occasion in
such a way that you are free to do just that. And as a
reward once it is all over, try my 'best nightcap'.

Six of the Best and a Nightcap

LANCASHIRE HOT POTS

HADDOCK FISH CAKES WITH TARTARE SAUCE

STEAK, KIDNEY AND MUSHROOM PIE

BOILED FILLET OF BEEF WITH CAPER SAUCE

BREAD AND BUTTER PUDDING

CHILLED SEMOLINA PUDDINGS

THE BEST NIGHT CAP IN THE WORLD

What do the 16 million foreign tourists who visit Britain look for? Of course, in the case of Americans and ex-colonials they come to trace their roots. Others come to discover the Highlands, Hebrides or Lakes.

But what of our food? I am certain the foreign visitor is looking (the great roast apart) for dishes such as a superlative steak and kidney pie, or an excellent hot pot, a creamy trifle with its real egg custard or a taste of a traditional bread and butter pudding. During the past decade we have learnt to approach eating with a view to health. Here, then, are six of our national dishes with new looks and bearing.

LANCASHIRE HOT POTS

SERVES 6

2 whole lamb fillets, trimmed and skinned
2 tablespoons olive or soy oil for frying
24 button onions, skinned
3 inner stalks celery, finely diced
18 button mushrooms
25 g (1 oz) pearl barley
salt
freshly ground black pepper
150 ml (¼ pint) dry white wine
450 ml (¾ pint) chicken stock
6 potatoes, each 100 g (4 oz) in weight, peeled and finely sliced
25 g (1 oz) melted butter

PREPARATION TIME: 30 minutes
COOKING TIME: about 2½ hours
OVEN: 170°C, 325°F, Gas Mark 3;
then: 190°C, 375°F, Gas Mark 5

I wondered whether I was taking a severe liberty with this one: the result, I think, proves I was not!

1 Have ready 6 ovenproof pots, approximately 400 ml (⅔ pint) size. Cut each fillet into 12 discs. Heat a little of the oil to smoking point. Quickly fry the lamb in small batches to seal and colour the meat. Place 4 pieces in each pot.

2 Brown the onions over a fairly fierce heat, adding a splash more oil if necessary. Lift them out with a draining spoon and divide between the pots. Do the same with the celery, mushrooms and pearl barley. A high heat and speed is best.

3 Season the contents of each pot lightly with a dredge of salt and 2–3 twists of the pepper mill. Pour over enough wine and stock to cover.

4 Arrange the potatoes neatly in overlapping circles on top of each and brush with melted butter. Season lightly with salt and pepper. Cover and cook in the preheated oven for 1½ hours. Take off the lids, raise the temperature and cook for a further 20–30 minutes, or until the potatoes are golden-brown.

All the elements of the traditional fish cake are brought together here, but the ingredients are all raw. The result is a remarkable renaissance for this favourite dish. You can serve the fish cakes with lemon wedges for breakfast or, accompanied by my new enriched tartare sauce, they are good for brunch or for a dinner-time starter.

1 Put the fish, eggs, potato, bread, salt and pepper into a blender or food processor and blend to a fine purée, adding the cream last of all so that it isn't overworked. For an extra fine texture, rub the mixture through a fine sieve. The mixture should be softish.

2 Have ready a jug of cold water and a dessertspoon (for large cakes) or a teaspoon (for small ones). Scoop out spoonfuls on to a wetted work surface, dipping the spoon in water each time. Using a wetted knife or palette knife, level and shape the cakes which should be about 1 cm ($\frac{1}{2}$ inch) thick.

3 Heat 2–3 tablespoons of clarified butter or soy oil in a skillet or frying pan to smoking point. Lift and slide the cakes into the smoking oil in batches of 5 or 6. Turn them after $\frac{1}{2}$ minute, when a golden crust will have formed. Lower the heat and cook them for 3–4 minutes. Drain on paper towels. Add a little more oil or butter when required.

4 To prepare the sauce, separate the yolk from the white of the hard-boiled egg. Chop the white and sieve the yolk on to a saucer.

5 Mix the mayonnaise to the texture of double cream with a little lemon juice or water, then add the Tabasco.

6 Stir in the sieved yolk, retaining a spoonful to sprinkle over as a garnish if you like, then mix in the remaining ingredients. Cover with cling film and chill ready for use.

HADDOCK FISH CAKES WITH TARTARE SAUCE

SERVES 5–6

450 g (1 lb) fresh haddock, filleted, skinned and boned
2 eggs, beaten
225 g (8 oz) raw potato, peeled and cubed into cold water
2 slices white bread, crustless, cut into small squares
salt
freshly ground black pepper
65 ml (2$\frac{1}{2}$ fl oz) single cream
clarified butter or soy oil for frying

FOR THE SAUCE:

1 hard-boiled egg, shelled and halved
300 ml ($\frac{1}{2}$ pint) mayonnaise
a little lemon juice or water
1–2 dashes of Tabasco sauce
4–5 American cocktail gherkins, finely chopped
1 tablespoon chives, finely snipped (or parsley or other green herb)
25 g (1 oz) prawns, chopped
3–4 anchovy fillets, separated and diced

PREPARATION TIME: 40 minutes
COOKING TIME: 20–30 minutes

VARIATION
For added luxury, a large peeled 'crevette' or American shrimp tail can be pressed into the mixture, and half a clove of crushed garlic plus 2 tablespoons of finely chopped fresh parsley can also be added. The cakes are delicious served cold, sliced and dressed with oil and vinegar or mayonnaise, or with the tartare sauce.

LEFT TO RIGHT: Lancashire hot pot; Haddock fish cakes with tartare sauce

STEAK, KIDNEY AND MUSHROOM PIE

SERVES 6

50 g (2 oz) butter or soy oil for frying
12 button onions, skinned
1 kg (2 lb) best steak, trimmed of all fat and sinew and cubed
2 teaspoons white flour
salt
freshly ground black pepper
225 g (8 oz) tiny button mushrooms
1 garlic clove, cut in half
225 g (8 oz) veal or lamb kidney (not ox)
2 sprigs fresh thyme

FOR THE CRUST:
150 g (5 oz) self-raising flour
1 level teaspoon baking powder
1 tablespoon finely grated lemon rind
1 level teaspoon salt
freshly ground white pepper
75 g (3 oz) cold, hard butter, coarsely grated
1 tablespoon finely chopped fresh parsley
1 egg beaten with 2 tablespoons cold water

PREPARATION TIME: 30 minutes
COOKING TIME: 3–3½ hours
OVEN: 190°C, 375°F, Gas Mark 5

1 Heat the oil or butter in a frying pan until it is lightly smoking and brown the onions. Transfer to a flame-proof casserole using a slotted spoon. Toss the meat in the flour and lightly brown it in the pan. Add to the casserole. Season sparingly with salt and a very little pepper, then mix in the mushrooms and the garlic.

2 Cut the kidney into 5 mm (¼ inch) slices and seal them in the pan; add to the casserole with the thyme.

3 Pour over enough water just to cover – 600 ml (1 pint) at most. Cover and simmer over a low heat for an hour, or cook in the preheated oven. Cool, then pour into a 1.5–1.75 litre (2–3 pint) pudding basin.

4 To make the crust, sift the flour, baking powder and seasonings into a bowl. Rub in the butter until the mixture resembles breadcrumbs. Sprinkle over the parsley. Add the egg and water to make a softish dough.

5 Turn on to a floured surface and press or roll into a circle which will just fit *inside* the top of the basin. Cover with greaseproof paper, then with foil – make a deep pleat and tie down well.

6 Place in a large saucepan one third filled with boiling water, cover and steam at a steady roll for 1½–2 hours. Serve a wedge of pastry with a spoonful of filling.

CLOCKWISE FROM THE TOP: Bread and butter pudding; Boiled fillet of beef with caper sauce; Steak, kidney and mushroom pie

BOILED FILLET OF BEEF WITH CAPER SAUCE

SERVES 6

1 × 750 g–1 kg (1½–2 lb) piece of fillet steak
1 garlic clove, cut into the thinnest slivers
small bunch of chives, whole
(2 pints) rich beef stock (page 21) or use canned consommé
6 young leeks, trimmed and cut in half
3 tomatoes, halved
6 cauliflower florets
12 whole young carrots, or older ones cut into sticks
1 celery heart, cut into 6
12 button onions

RICH CAPER SAUCE:
4 egg yolks, (size 1)
50 g (2 oz) butter, at room temperature and cut into small cubes
2 tablespoons sweet capers, drained
1 tablespoon snipped chives
2 teaspoons lemon juice
salt
freshly ground black pepper

GARNISH:
1 tablespoon each chopped chives and flat-leafed parsley

PREPARATION TIME: 50 minutes
COOKING TIME: 15–25 minutes

1 Choose a pan just large enough to hold the piece of fillet steak, which should be rolled and tied securely at 2.5 cm (1 inch) intervals. Use a sharp pointed knife to stab the steak, at least 4 cm (1½ inches) deep. Leave the knife in place and gently press it back to slide 1 sliver of garlic and 2 or 3 whole chives into the incision. Do this 6 or so times down the length of the fillet.

2 Bring the stock to boiling point, lower in the fillet, reduce the heat, and simmer for 10 minutes for rare, 20 minutes for more well done. (It takes remarkably little time to cook!)

3 Remove the steak from the stock, cut away the strings and put into a deep serving dish, cover and keep warm. Bring the stock back to boiling point and put the vegetables in to cook for 3–4 minutes, leaving them still crisp. Remove with a draining spoon and put round the meat with a ladleful or two of the stock.

4 To make the sauce, strain 300 ml (½ pint) of the stock into a basin arranged over a pan of gently boiling water and whisk in the egg yolks until thick and the whisk leaves a distinct trail. Remove the basin from the heat and briskly whisk in the softened butter. Do not reheat. Stir in the capers, chives and lemon juice, then taste and adjust the seasoning. Pour into a warm sauceboat.

5 Carve the meat into 5 mm (¼ inch) slices, sprinkle over the herbs and serve with some of the vegetables and the sauce. The best accompaniment is plenty of tiny Jersey potatoes tossed in butter and lightly sprinkled with nutmeg.

BREAD AND BUTTER PUDDING

SERVES 6–8

50 g (2 oz) softened unsalted butter
175 g (6 oz) seedless raisins or sultanas, soaked overnight in 2–3 tablespoons of sherry, whisky, brandy or gin
8 thin slices of good white bread, crusts removed
100 g (4 oz) sieved apricot jam
3 eggs (size 1), beaten with 2 extra egg yolks
50 g (2 oz) caster sugar
300 ml (½ pint) rich milk
1 teaspoon vanilla essence or pod
300 ml (½ pint) double cream
icing sugar

PREPARATION TIME: 30 minutes, plus soaking overnight and resting
COOKING TIME: 50–60 minutes
OVEN: 160°C, 325°F, Gas Mark 3

1 Butter a 23–25 cm (9–10 inch) diameter ovenproof dish, 4–5 cm (1½–2 inches) deep, with a little unsalted butter. Scatter the soaked raisins evenly over the bottom.

2 Use the rest of the butter to spread on the bread and make 4 large sandwiches with the apricot jam. Cut each one into 6 pieces or circles with a small cutter. Arrange these, overlapping if necessary, around the edge of the dish.

3 Beat the eggs and yolks with the sugar. Bring the milk, vanilla and cream to the boil (slowly if you have a pod, so that the essence is extracted from it).

4 Remove the pod if used, then pour the hot liquid into the egg mixture and mix well with a balloon whisk.

5 Ladle the custard over the bread pieces, so that they are soaked but not displaced. Leave for 10 minutes.

6 Place the dish in a bain-marie large enough to contain it without the water overflowing into the pudding. Bake in a preheated oven for 45–60 minutes or until the custard is just set and the bread lightly browned.

7 Dredge with icing sugar. For added effect and flavour, caramelize the top under a very hot grill. Serve with double pouring cream.

CHILLED SEMOLINA PUDDINGS

SERVES 8

450 ml ($\frac{3}{4}$ pint) single cream
2 tablespoons caster sugar (or to taste)
1 teaspoon finely grated zest of 1 orange
25 g (1 oz) semolina
1 teaspoon gelatine crystals, dissolved in 1 tablespoon cold water
4 egg yolks, beaten
300 ml ($\frac{1}{2}$ pint) double cream
knob of softened, unsalted butter for greasing
8 apricot halves, blanched (or fresh, or tinned)

APRICOT SAUCE:
350 g (12 oz) fresh or drained tinned apricots, pitted
sugar, if needed
1 tablespoon lemon juice
1 tablespoon apricot liqueur or Grand Marnier
sprigs of mint, to decorate

PREPARATION TIME: 30 minutes, plus cooling and chilling
COOKING TIME: about 10 minutes

1 In a non-stick pan bring the single cream, sugar and zest slowly to the boil, then sprinkle in the semolina, reduce the heat and simmer for 3–4 minutes.

2 Remove from the heat and, whilst still hot, add the softened gelatine and the egg yolks, mixing in well. Leave to cool.

3 Whip the double cream just to the ribbon stage, then cut into the mixture.

4 Lightly butter 8 individual moulds (use coffee cups if you don't have a set of tin ones). Put an apricot half in the bottom of each, curved side down. Fill with the semolina mixture, then chill.

5 To make the sauce, purée the apricots in a blender or food processor, then rub through a fine-meshed sieve. Add the remaining ingredients and chill.

6 To turn the semolina puddings out of the moulds, ease the edge with your finger, then dip each tin for a couple of seconds into a basin of boiling water and wipe dry. Pour the chilled apricot sauces on to 8 individual plates, then turn out the semolina puddings on top and decorate.

THE BEST NIGHT CAP IN THE WORLD

2 heaped teaspoons malted milk drink
25 ml (1 fl oz) brandy or whisky
200 ml ($\frac{1}{3}$ pint) boiling milk
pinch of cocoa powder or grated chocolate

PREPARATION TIME: 3 minutes, plus boiling the milk

1 Mix the malted milk drink to a smooth paste with the brandy using a fork.

2 Slowly pour over the boiling milk whisking well with the fork to eliminate lumps. Sprinkle with cocoa powder or chocolate and it's ready to drink.

Easter Lunch with a Difference

A PASTY OF SALMON IN RED WINE WITH CREAMED MUSHROOMS AND PLUMS

EASTER TERRINE WITH HONEY-MINT SAUCE

PECORINO, CUCUMBER, TOMATO AND ORANGE SALAD (WITH ANCHOVIES)

HOT PINEAPPLE IN SAUTERNE WITH SHAVED ALMONDS

As I have already stated, the element of surprise is all-important in any kind of entertaining. Start with a *hot* fish course, followed by a marvellous *cold* turkey terrine in which turkey forcemeat is wrapped up in smoked salmon – a luxurious treat for Easter. An exotically colourful salad accompanies this dish, though you could serve buttered new potatoes if you prefer. Finally, my luncheon menu is rounded off with a festive pineapple dish, which comes to the table hot as a surprise finale to this deliciously different Easter Sunday meal.

A PASTY OF SALMON IN RED WINE WITH CREAMED MUSHROOMS AND PLUMS

SERVES 6

1 × 350 g (12 oz) packet frozen puff pastry, thawed
1 egg, beaten
25 g (1 oz) butter
175 g (6 oz) button mushrooms, quartered
2 tablespoons Madeira or medium dry sherry
salt
freshly ground black pepper
1 teaspoon ground mace
½ bottle red Burgundy-type wine
½ stock cube
juice of 1 lemon
100 ml (3½ fl oz) cream
4 plums
225 g (8 oz) middle-cut salmon, wild or farm, skinned
1 egg yolk, (size 1)

PREPARATION TIME: 50 minutes, plus chilling
COOKING TIME: 1–1¼ hours
OVEN: 230°C, 450°F, Gas Mark 8;
then: 190°C, 375°F, Gas Mark 5;
finally: 140°C, 275°F, Gas Mark 1

1 First make the pasties. Roll out the pastry evenly to an oblong approximately 20 × 30 cm (8 × 12 inches) and 1 cm (⅓ inch) thick. Cut into 6 squares approximately 10 × 10 cm (4 × 4 inches). Do not drag the knife when cutting, as this impedes the rising of the pastry.

2 Lift the squares on to a wetted baking sheet. Brush the tops with beaten egg. Be careful to avoid getting any on the side edges, as this, too, will impede rising. Score the top with the blade of a knife, then chill for 1 hour.

3 Bake in a preheated oven for 15 minutes, then reduce the heat and continue for a further 15 minutes. The pastry should be crisp right through. Cool on a wire tray, then carefully split in half. Ⓐ

4 Heat the butter until almondy. Add the mushrooms and fry over a brisk heat for 2–3 minutes. Add the Madeira or sherry and simmer for a further 2–3 minutes. Season well with salt, pepper and ground mace. Transfer to a liquidizer or food processor and purée finely.

5 Put the red wine and stock cube in a saucepan and reduce to 200 ml (⅓ pint) by boiling them together rapidly. Add 1 teaspoon of the lemon juice. Add 65 ml (2½ fl oz) of the cream and bubble until the sauce is cohered and the consistency of pouring cream. Season carefully.

6 Stone the plums, cut into slices and heat through in a shallow ovenproof dish, without liquid but seasoned lightly with salt and pepper.

7 Cut the salmon into 12 × 5 mm (¼ inch) thick slivers along the grain. Bring 2.5 cm (1 inch) lightly salted water and the remainder of the lemon juice to simmering point in a shallow pan. Poach the slivers of salmon for 2 minutes. Lift out carefully with a fish slice and drain on paper towels, while keeping the fish on the slice.

8 Stand the pastry bases and lids on a baking sheet and warm through in the oven at the lowest temperature for 10–15 minutes. Put each pastry base on a dinner plate with a pool of red wine sauce and 1 or 2 plum slices.

9 Just before serving, boil the mushroom purée rapidly. Mix with the egg yolk with the remaining cream. Remove the pan from the heat, stir in the egg and cream to thicken the purée slightly. Divide the mixture evenly between the pasty bases. Top each pasty with 2 pieces of salmon, dribble over a little wine sauce and add the pasty lids. *Pictured overleaf.*

Ⓐ The pasties can be baked 2–3 days in advance and stored in an airtight container.

EASTER TERRINE WITH HONEY-MINT SAUCE

SERVES 6–8

275 g (10 oz) salmon (weighed after skinning and boning),
cut into 2.5 cm (1 inch) pieces
4 tablespoons whisky
1 tablespoon lemon juice
salt
freshly ground white pepper
2 eggs (size 3, 4)
300 ml ($\frac{1}{2}$ pint) double cream
olive oil for greasing
450 g (1 lb) smoked salmon, thinly sliced
$\frac{1}{4}$ teaspoon ground mace
450–750 g (1–1$\frac{1}{2}$ lb) turkey breast, boned and cubed
100 g (4 oz) pistachio nuts, roughly crushed

SAUCE:
175 ml (6 fl oz) single cream
1 dessertspoon acacia or other flavour blossom honey
2 tablespoons raspberry, redcurrant or red wine vinegar
$\frac{1}{2}$ teaspoon salt
freshly ground white pepper
1 tablespoon chopped fresh mint

PREPARATION TIME: 40 minutes, plus marinating and
chilling overnight
COOKING TIME: 1 hour
OVEN: 200°C, 400°F, Gas Mark 6

1 Marinate the salmon for 2 hours in the whisky and lemon juice, seasoned well with salt and white pepper. Chill the eggs and cream.

2 Brush the inside and edges of a 1 kg (4 lb) seamless loaf tin with oil. Fit a piece of oiled greaseproof in the base, then line with the smoked salmon.

3 Remove the salmon from the marinade and purée with the eggs in a food processor. Add 1 teaspoon of salt and the mace and pour in the cream in one slow *steady* stream, stopping when you have a stiffish purée. Transfer the purée to a large bowl. Mix in the turkey pieces, the remaining marinade and the nuts. Spoon into the terrine, filling the corners.

4 Fold over any smoked salmon 'flaps'. Cover the terrine with a lid or buttered foil and stand it in a tin or bain-marie of hot water.

5 Bake in a preheated oven for 1 hour. Cool. Cover with a piece of foil-covered board and press with a weight. Cover with cling film and chill overnight.

6 Mix all the sauce ingredients together in a basin using a small balloon whisk.

7 Unmould the terrine, remove the lining paper and serve cut into slices 1 cm ($\frac{1}{3}$ inch) thick, passing the sauce separately.

PECORINO, CUCUMBER, TOMATO AND ORANGE SALAD (WITH ANCHOVIES)

SERVES 6–8

DRESSING:
150 ml ($\frac{1}{4}$ pint) olive oil
juice and finely grated rind of 1 orange
1 teaspoon mild French mustard
salt
freshly ground black pepper
1 garlic clove, crushed (optional)
1 teaspoon caster sugar

SALAD:
225 g (8 oz) pecorino cheese, cut into cubes
2 beefsteak tomatoes, skinned, seeded and cut into 1 cm
($\frac{1}{2}$ inch) chunks
1 small cucumber, halved, seeded and cut into 1 cm ($\frac{1}{2}$ inch)
chunks

GARNISH:
1 dozen anchovy fillets
orange segments

PREPARATION TIME: 20 minutes

1 Put all the dressing ingredients into a screw-top jar and shake well.

2 Mix the salad ingredients together in a large bowl and chill.

3 Dress the salad just before serving. Garnish with anchovies and orange segments.

HOT PINEAPPLE IN SAUTERNE WITH SHAVED ALMONDS

SERVES 6–8

1 pineapple
50 g (2 oz) unsalted butter
50 g (2 oz) moist light brown sugar or caster sugar
$\frac{1}{2}$ bottle sweet white wine
1 teaspoon vanilla essence
75–100 g (3–4 oz) shaved or slivered almonds

PREPARATION TIME: 10 minutes
COOKING TIME: 10–12 minutes

1 Cut off the top and bottom of the pineapple. Remove the skin with a sharp, serrated knife, cutting away any stray bits. Cut the fruit in half from top to bottom. Remove the core by cutting a 'V' incision down either side of it and discard. Slice each half of the fruit into approximately 10 semi-circles.

2 Put the butter, sugar, wine and vanilla essence into a wide shallow pan, which must be meticulously clean. Simmer until syrupy, about 10 minutes.

CLOCKWISE FROM THE TOP: Easter terrine with honey mint sauce and Pecorino, cucumber, tomato and orange salad; A pasty of salmon in red wine; Hot pineapple in Sauterne

3 Add the pineapple pieces to this sauce and heat through for a minute or two, bubbling gently.

4 Transfer the fruit to a serving dish and sprinkle liberally with the almonds. Serve with ice cream or fresh cream if liked.

A Christmas Buffet

SMOKED SALMON MOUSSE(S) WITH RED CAVIAR

SPICED FRIED TURKEY BREAST IN WHITE WINE

SPROUT AND PEPPER SALAD

CHRISTMAS CRANBERRY TART

BEJEWELLED CHRISTMAS CHARLOTTE

PINEAPPLE AND STRAWBERRY SALAD WITH DRAMBUIE

*I*t seems almost impertinent to give yet more recipes for turkey and its attendant stuffings and so I shall resist.

The dishes I do give here for Christmas fare are for slotting in to those other areas where your imagination might let you down: ideas for starters, or for dishes to include in a Christmas buffet.

I have included some fruity desserts with a Christmasy feeling – not least because they're usually out of season and are being bought as a luxury normally not indulged in and I have given another treat in the form of a starter.

The Smoked Salmon Mousse appears (and is) costly, but it is *so* delicious that you won't mind spending a bit more – both money and time – to prepare it.

Any or all of my suggestions will work, either as part of a formal meal, or as a constituent of a festive buffet slotted in and amongst your own favourite buffet fare, or just to give that element of something special when the cold turkey comes out – yet again!

A happy Christmas.

SMOKED SALMON MOUSSE WITH RED CAVIAR

MAKES 6

FISH STOCK:
2 Dover Sole bones, well washed and broken up
1.2 litres (2 pints) cold water
1 good sprig of parsley
squeeze of lemon juice
pinch of dried thyme
300 ml ($\frac{1}{2}$ pint) dry white wine
1 dozen black peppercorns

MOUSSE:
1$\frac{1}{2}$ sachets gelatine crystals
350 g (12 oz) Scotch smoked salmon
1 × 50 g (2 oz) jar of red salmon caviar or lumpfish roe
500 ml (18 fl oz) double cream
salt
$\frac{1}{4}$ teaspoon freshly ground white pepper
juice of $\frac{1}{2}$ lemon
whipped cream (optional) to garnish

PREPARATION TIME: 45 minutes, plus chilling
COOKING TIME: 40–50 minutes

1 Bring all the stock ingredients to the boil in a large saucepan, reduce the heat and simmer for 30–40 minutes. Skim off any scum, then strain into a clean pan. Reduce by boiling to approximately 300 ml ($\frac{1}{2}$ pint).

2 Measure 300 ml ($\frac{1}{2}$ pint) of the boiling stock into a bowl, sprinkle over the gelatine crystals and whisk until completely dissolved. Allow to cool completely but do not allow to set.

3 Put the smoked salmon and a little of the stock into a food processor or liquidizer and make a fine purée. Be careful not to overprocess. Turn this mixture into a bowl adding the remaining cool fish stock. Fold in 40 g (1$\frac{1}{2}$ oz) of the caviar. Whip the cream, adding a little salt, the pepper and lemon juice, until it stands in firm but not too stiff peaks. (The cream peaks should *just* fall when drawn up with the whisk.)

4 Cut and fold the 2 mixtures together. Pour into a pretty serving dish or into individual ramekins fitted with collars. Make a collar for the ramekin with a double thickness of oiled greaseproof paper. Wrap around the dish, secure with a staple at the top and an elastic band round the waist. Chill until set, about 4 hours. Garnish with the remaining caviar and a blob of whipped cream.

CLOCKWISE FROM THE TOP: Sprout and pepper salad; Spiced fried turkey breast in white wine; Smoked salmon mousse with red caviar

SPICED FRIED TURKEY BREAST IN WHITE WINE WITH GRAPEFRUIT AND GRAPES

SERVES 8

1 × 4.5 kg (10 lb) self-basting turkey
1 tablespoon olive oil
1 tablespoon butter
salt
freshly ground black pepper
1 teaspoon mace
3 pink grapefruits, knife-segmented
225 g (8 oz) seedless or seeded green grapes
¼ bottle dry white wine
2 teaspoons ground coriander
16 whole cherry tomatoes or 4 ordinary tomatoes, halved

PREPARATION TIME: 30 minutes
COOKING TIME: about 30 minutes

1 Remove the breasts from the turkey. Reserve the legs for use in a curry or fricassée on some other occasion.

2 Heat the oil and butter in a skillet or frying pan large enough to contain the 2 breasts side by side. When the oils are smoking, seal the breasts for 1 minute on each side, or until golden-brown. Season well with salt, pepper and mace. Reduce the heat and continue frying the breasts until cooked, about 6 minutes on each side, turning them at 2 minute intervals. Remove to a warm serving dish.

3 Strain the juices into a clean frying pan. Add the grapefruit and grapes, cover with the wine and season well with salt, pepper and the coriander. Heat through then remove the fruits to the serving dish with a slotted spoon. Add the tomatoes and let the pan juices bubble until you have 150 ml (¼ pint) viscous sauce.

4 Carve each turkey breast into 8 thickish diagonal slices and spoon over the wine sauce.

SPROUT AND PEPPER SALAD

SERVES 5–6

350 g (12 oz) small sprouts
2 large red peppers, cleaned and seeded

DRESSING:
juice of 1 lemon, made up to 150 ml (¼ pint) with olive oil
1 teaspoon mild French mustard
salt
freshly ground black pepper
sprigs of flat-leaved parsley, to garnish

PREPARATION TIME: 15 minutes

1 Clean the sprouts and shred with the peppers on the slicing blade of a food processor. (The vegetables must be thread fine.) Mix the dressing ingredients together, pour over the shredded vegetables and toss well. Garnish and serve.

CHRISTMAS CRANBERRY TART

SERVES 8–10

150 g (5 oz) plain white flour
1 tablespoon icing sugar
75 g (3 oz) hard butter, cut into dice
1 tablespoon lemon juice
1 egg yolk
350 g (12 oz) cranberries, fresh or frozen
juice of 1 orange
50 g (2 oz) caster sugar
25 ml (1 fl oz) rum or whisky

TOPPING:

75 g (3 oz) unsalted butter (softened)
150 g (5 oz) caster sugar
2 eggs, beaten
1 heaped teaspoon grated orange rind
150 g (5 oz) ground almonds
25 g (1 oz) plain white flour

PREPARATION TIME: 45 minutes, plus resting and
chilling
COOKING TIME: 45 minutes
OVEN: 200°C, 400°F, Gas Mark 6;
then: 180°C, 350°F, Gas Mark 4

1 Sieve the flour and icing sugar together. Rub in the butter until sandy textured. Mix the lemon juice, 1 tablespoon water and the egg yolks together, then add to the flour mixture to bind. Gather into a ball, but be careful that you do not overwork the pastry. Leave to relax for 30 minutes or more.

2 Roll out the pastry and use it to line a 20–23 cm (8–9 inch) loose-bottomed flan tin, 4 cm (1¼ inches) deep. Chill again. Line the pastry with buttered foil, fill with dried beans and bake blind for about 15 minutes. Remove the foil and beans.

3 Wash the cranberries well. Simmer over the lowest heat with orange juice until they 'pop' and are soft. Add the caster sugar and rum or whisky, then mash to a purée. Spread over the bottom of the cooked flan case (still in the metal tin) leaving behind some of the juices.

4 To make the topping. Cream the butter and sugar well. Incorporate the eggs gradually and add the orange rind. Sieve in the almonds and flour, fold in, then spread over the cranberry sauce.

5 Reduce the temperature and bake for 45 minutes. The pastry should be lovely and crisp. Serve hot or cool (not chilled), with whipped cream.

BEJEWELLED CHRISTMAS CHARLOTTE

SERVES 8–10

2 packets langues de chats or boudoir biscuits
1 egg white, beaten
225 g (8 oz) unsalted butter, softened
175 g (6 oz) icing sugar, sieved
25 ml (1 fl oz) rum, brandy, Kirsch, or other liqueur
5 egg yolks
100 g (4 oz) glacé cherries, roughly chopped
100 g (4 oz) glacé pineapple, roughly chopped
300 g (11 oz) walnuts

DECORATION:

300 ml (½ pint) double cream
25 g (1 oz) icing sugar
2 tablespoons liqueur (as above)
crystallized rose petals, violets or other glacé fruits

PREPARATION TIME: 30 minutes, plus chilling overnight

This sweet is very rich, so should be served in thin slices. I often make mine in an oblong tin or mould as it is easier to control the size of slice this way. Cut with a knife dipped in hot water.

1 Line a 15–18 cm (6–7 inch) charlotte mould, basin or loaf tin with langues de chats or boudoir biscuits, trimming off any excess biscuit tips. To help line the mould it is a good idea to touch one side of each biscuit lightly with beaten egg white as you fit them together.

2 Cream the butter and sugar together until white. Beat in the liqueur and egg yolks and mix in the glacé fruits. Place 150 g (5 oz) of the nuts in a blender or processor and pulverize. Roughly crush 50 g (2 oz) of the remaining nuts. Mix both quantities into the charlotte mixture. Spoon and press the mixture into the lined mould. Then chill overnight.

3 Whip the cream with the sugar and liqueur. Turn out the charlotte and decorate with the cream, the crystallized flowers or fruits and remaining walnuts.

PINEAPPLE AND STRAWBERRY SALAD WITH DRAMBUIE

CLOCKWISE FROM THE TOP: Bejewelled Christmas charlotte; Christmas cranberry tart; Pineapple and strawberry salad with Drambuie

SERVES 6–8

450 g (1 lb) strawberries
1 small pineapple
50 g (2 oz) caster sugar
juice of 1 lemon
120 ml (4 fl oz) Drambuie

PREPARATION TIME: 30 minutes, plus chilling

1 Quarter the strawberries. Peel and core the pineapple, then cut into 1 cm ($\frac{1}{2}$ inch) thick strips and finally into 1 cm ($\frac{1}{2}$ inch) pieces. Dredge with caster sugar.

2 Toss the pineapple and strawberries in the lemon juice and liqueur and chill well before serving.

A Wedding Reception for Forty

CHAMPAGNE 'ROYALE'

KOULIBIAC OF SALMON AND SOLE

ROAST STUFFED BONED DUCKLING

POTATO AND EGG SALAD WITH SOUR CREAM DRESSING

GREEN BEANS VINAIGRETTE

TOMATO SALAD WITH ORANGE YOGURT DRESSING

18TH CENTURY RATAFIA TRIFLE

RICH VELVET CHOCOLATE CREAMS

More and more brides are wanting to have their wedding reception at home, where they feel at ease against a familiar background and I can think of no better place to have such a small-scale celebratory party. I know, as I have two daughters-in-law who wanted things that way.

One way of coping with such an occasion is to have a champagne party serving a selection of the more substantial cocktail food given on pages 90–97. However, for a grander occasion providing more of a meal, I have devised the following menu. Choose a canapé, such as 'Gravadlax on Bread' (page 86), to serve with the Champagne 'Royale'.

A checklist of things you will need, a countdown of activities and advice on how to go about it all are given on pages 8 to 9.

CHAMPAGNE ROYALE

30 bottles Champagne or dry sparkling wine
3 × 3 kg (7 lb) bags of ice cubes
3 bottles Framboise or Cassis liqueur or blackcurrant cordial, chilled
40 strawberries with stalks, about 1.75 kg (4 lb)

PREPARATION TIME: 30 minutes

Begin your reception with a real sparkling splash of style with this exotic cocktail, accompanied by one of the canapés on page 86. Allow three-quarters of a bottle of Champagne per head.

1 Place 2 thoroughly cleaned plastic dustbins outside in the shade or garage. Put as many champagne bottles as will stand upright in the bottom of each. Pack ice cubes round them. Put in another layer of bottles, inverted, and cover with more ice. Lay the top layer horizontally across the other bottles and pile the remaining ice cubes on top. Ⓐ

2 An hour before serving, place $\frac{1}{2}$–1 tablespoon of liquer in each glass. Splice the strawberries from the base but leave still joined at the top. Place a strawberry over the rim of each glass.

3 When ready to serve, remove the Champagne bottles, 6 at a time, and use to top up the glasses.

Ⓐ This can be done at least 4 hours in advance.

KOULIBIAC OF SALMON AND SOLE

SERVES 40

FILLING:
1.5 kg (3 lb) salmon (tail piece will do)
1.5 kg (3 lb) Dover sole fillets, or other white fish, such as
turbot, monkfish, halibut or haddock
50 g (2 oz) butter
450 g (1 lb) button mushrooms, quartered
175 ml (6 fl oz) brandy
600 ml (1 pint) double cream
4 tablespoons flour
2 teaspoons mild French mustard
4 tablespoons chopped fresh tarragon, or 4 teaspoons
reconstituted dried
salt
freshly ground black pepper
450 g (1 lb) long-grain rice
1.2 litres (2 pints) fish or chicken stock (use 2 stock cubes)
fresh herbs, to garnish

PASTRY CASE:
4 × 350 g (12 oz) and 2 × 225 g (8 oz) packets frozen puff
pastry, thawed
2 egg yolks beaten with 150 ml (¼ pint) cream
1.5 litres (2½ pints) Mayonnaise (page 23), to serve

PREPARATION TIME: 1 hour
COOKING TIME: about 1 hour
OVEN: 220°C, 425°F, Gas Mark 7

1 First make the filling, skin, bone and cut the salmon and Dover sole into 1 cm (½ inch) cubes. Melt the butter in a large 2.25 litre (4 pint) saucepan, and, when foaming, toss in the mushrooms and fish and fry over a brisk heat for about 2 minutes. Drain off and reserve any liquid produced. Warm the brandy, pour over the mixture and allow to ignite.

2 Using a balloon whisk, mix the double cream with the flour and reserved liquid in a bowl, then pour into the mixture in the pan to quench the flames. Stir in the mustard and tarragon. Season well with salt and pepper and simmer gently for 2–3 minutes only. Allow to cool completely.

3 Boil the rice in the stock for 20 minutes. Drain the rice, reserving the remaining stock. Mix the rice and fish mixture together in a large bowl. Add salt and pepper to taste. The mixture should be softish but just hold its shape. Chill. Ⓐ

4 To make the pastry case, roll out the four 350 g (12 oz) packets of puff pastry to sheets approximately the same size as 2 of your baking tins or trays. Invert the tins and lay one sheet of pastry on top of each. (The tin is inverted to help remove the pastry when baked.) Brush all over with some of the egg and cream mixture. Place the remaining 2 sheets of pastry to one side.

5 Roll out each of the 225 g (8 oz) packets of puff pastry to a rectangle 23 × 13 cm (9 × 5 inches). Cut a paper template into the shape of a fish, place on top of one of the rectangles and cut out a pastry fish shape. Next cut out a small ring, 1 cm (½ inch) in diameter, for the eye. Brush all over with the egg and cream mixture. Using a teaspoon, make indentations to look like fish scales. Repeat with the other piece of pastry.

6 Pile half the prepared fish mixture on to one of the pastry bases, spreading to within 1 cm (½ inch) of the edge. Lay a large sheet of pastry over the fish mixture. Press the edges well together. Crimp and knock up the edges. Place one of the fish-shaped pastries firmly on top. Clip 2 steam holes with scissors. Brush with the egg and cream mixture any parts which have been missed. Repeat with the remaining fish mixture. Ⓐ

7 Bake in a preheated oven for 30 minutes, and leave to cool. Garnish and serve with mayonnaise.

Ⓐ The filling can be made 1 day in advance, covered and kept chilled. The whole koulibiac can be assembled the day before and kept chilled.

Champagne royale; Koulibiac of salmon

ROAST STUFFED BONED DUCK

SERVES 16–20

4 tablespoons butter, soy or olive oil
450 g (1 lb) gammon, finely diced
450 g (1 lb) celery, cut into small dice
2 eggs (size 1)
450 g (1 lb) chicken breast, skinned and boned
450 g (1 lb) sausagemeat
4 tablespoons chopped fresh sage
2 tablespoons rubbed fresh thyme leaves or 4 teaspoons dried
sage and 2 teaspoons dried thyme
450 g (1 lb) black pudding or salami, cut into cubes
450 g (1 lb) hazelnuts or walnuts, crushed
450 g (1 lb) dried apricots, soaked, drained and diced
2 teaspoons freshly ground black pepper
salt
2 × 5–6 lb ducks, boned

PREPARATION TIME: 30 minutes, plus soaking overnight
COOKING TIME: 1½–1¾ hours
OVEN: 200°C, 400°F, Gas Mark 6

The stuffing I give you here has a rich, almost gamy flavour. A small capon could be used instead of the duck.

1 Heat the butter or oil in a large frying pan and quickly fry the gammon until nicely browned. Remove with a draining spoon to a plate. In the residue fats and over a medium heat, fry the celery without colouring too much. Add to the ham and leave to cool.

2 Purée the egg, chicken and sausagemeat in a food processor. Add the herbs halfway through. Scrape into a large bowl, then mix in the black pudding or salami, nuts and apricots, together with any residue oil. Add the pepper and a little salt. The mixture should be softish.

3 Spread out one of the boned ducks and clip away any stray pieces of bone and sinew. Pile half the stuffing in the centre of the meat, spreading it out just a little. Wrap over the skin and re-form as best you can into a duck shape. Once the stuffing is completely contained, you can shape the duck with your hands.

4 Thread a large needle with *linen* thread. Sew the skin together – again as best you can – but making sure there are no holes and piercing the skin about 2.5 cm (1 inch) away from the edge. If there are any holes, then darn these! Season the skin with salt and pepper. *Do not prick the skin.*

5 Turn the duck right way up, shaping it with your hands. Now, either pull a piece of butcher's knitted tubing over the duck like a stocking, or take a long metal skewer and push this right through the centre of one leg and out through the centre of the other leg on the other side, and tie the duck at 8 cm (3 inch) intervals with string. Repeat with the other duck.

6 Place a wide strip of foil on the racks of your roasting tins and stand the ducks on this. Roast in a preheated oven for 1½–1¾ hours. If roasting on different shelves, change the position of the 2 tins half-way through; if roasting side by side drop the temperature to 190°C, 375°F, Gas Mark 5 and increase the cooking time by 20 minutes. Leave to cool. Ⓐ Serve, in 3 mm (⅛ inch) thick slices.

Ⓐ Roast the ducks the evening before your party, so that the flesh is succulent. Cover and keep chilled. Bring to room temperature before serving.

POTATO AND EGG SALAD WITH SOUR CREAM DRESSING

SERVES 20–24

2.25 kg (5 lb) waxy new potatoes, boiled and skinned after
cooking
3 glasses dry white wine
6 tablespoons olive oil
salt
freshly ground black pepper
900 ml (1½ pints) soured cream
3 heaped teaspoons mild French mustard
juice of 1¼ lemons, strained
2 teaspoons caster sugar
1 teaspoon salt
8 hard-boiled eggs, roughly chopped

GARNISH:
2 bunches watercress, picked and washed
20 mint leaves, shredded
8 hard-boiled eggs, yolks only (from Green Beans
Vinaigrette), optional

PREPARATION TIME: 45 minutes
COOKING TIME: 20–30 minutes (for potatoes)

Cook the potatoes in 2 batches for ease of handling.

1 Cut the warm potatoes into 8 mm (⅓ inch) dice. Mix the wine and oil together, then splash over the potatoes and season them liberally with salt and pepper. Leave to cool and absorb the dressing. Ⓐ

2 Mix the cream, mustard, lemon juice, sugar and 1 teaspoon of salt together in a large plastic washing-up bowl. Carefully fold in the potatoes and chopped eggs.

3 Pile on to 2 large platters. Garnish with watercress sprigs and mint and sprinkle with a veil of the sieved hard-boiled egg yolk (if used).

Ⓐ The potatoes can be dressed up to 1 day beforehand. The garnishes can be prepared the day before and stored in plastic bags or tubs in the refrigerator.

GREEN BEANS VINAIGRETTE

SERVES 20–24

1.75 kg (4 lb) French, stick, or Kenya beans, topped, tailed and stringed
chicken stock, to cover (use stock cubes)

DRESSING:
225 g (8 oz) onion, finely chopped
8 hard-boiled eggs, whites only, finely chopped (reserve the yolks for Potato and Egg Salad)
18 cocktail gherkins, finely chopped
4 tablespoons fresh parsley, finely chopped
4 tablespoons chives, finely chopped
600 ml (1 pint) vinaigrette (page 23)

PREPARATION TIME: 1 hour (with a helping hand)
COOKING TIME: 15 minutes (including eggs)

1 Cut the beans into sticks, all about 5 cm (2 inches) long. Boil in chicken stock for 2–3 minutes only. Drain, cool and chill. (Keep overnight, if liked.)

2 Place all the dressing ingredients into a bowl and mix well together.

3 The night before, arrange the beans in a large circle on 2 large platters. Cover with cling film. A One hour before serving, spoon over the dressing.

CLOCKWISE FROM THE TOP: Tomato salad with orange yogurt dressing; Green beans vinaigrette; Roast stuffed boned duck; Potato and egg salad with sour cream dressing

TOMATO SALAD WITH ORANGE YOGURT DRESSING

SERVES 20–24

DRESSING:
300 ml ($\frac{1}{2}$ pint) olive oil
150 ml ($\frac{1}{4}$ pint) red wine vinegar
300 ml ($\frac{1}{2}$ pint) plain unsweetened yogurt
4 garlic cloves, crushed
4 heaped teaspoons mild French mustard
finely grated peel of 2 oranges
16–18 large beefsteak tomatoes, stalks pulled out

PREPARATION TIME: 45 minutes

1 Place all the dressing ingredients in a bowl and mix well together. (Make 3 days in advance, if liked.)

2 Make a cross incision across the base of each tomato. Skin them by plunging them 2 at a time into a pan of boiling water until you see the skin just starting to curl back, about 15 seconds. With a draining spoon, transfer them to a sink of cold water. Drain and remove the skins.

3 Slice thinly, arrange in concentric circles or rows on 2 large platters and cover with cling film. A Spoon the dressing over just before serving.

139

18TH CENTURY RATAFIA TRIFLE

4 packets trifle sponges
2 × 350 g (12 oz) jars apricot jam
2 packets ratafia biscuits, crumbled
300 ml (½ pint) medium dry Madeira or Amontillado sherry

CUSTARD:
12 egg yolks
2 teaspoons cornflour
600 ml (1 pint) milk
600 ml (1 pint) single cream
2 teaspoons vanilla extract
about 75 g (3 oz) caster sugar
300 ml (½ pint) double cream, whipped to soft peak

TOPPING:
1.2 litres (2 pints) double cream
85 ml (3 fl oz) brandy or medium dry sherry
50 g (2 oz) caster sugar
4 packets ratafia biscuits
225 g (8 oz) blanched split almonds
8 glacé apricots, or pineapple
angelica pieces

PREPARATION TIME: 1½ hours
COOKING TIME: 15 minutes

1 Split the trifle sponges in half, spread with jam and sandwich together again. Cut into cubes. Ⓐ

2 Arrange a layer of these cubes in each of two 2 litre (3–4 pint) serving bowls. Add a layer of ratafias and splash liberally with Maderia or sherry. Continue in this way until the bowls are filled.

3 Using a balloon whisk, whisk the yolks and cornflour in a large bowl until smooth, pale and creamy.

4 Heat the milk, single cream, vanilla extract and 75 g (3 oz) sugar to boiling point in a non-stick pan, stirring from time to time. Pour over the egg mixture whisking briskly, then strain back into the rinsed-out pan.

5 Return the custard to a minimal heat and, *stirring* with a balloon whisk, allow the custard to thicken. As soon as it does so, stand the pan in a sink containing 10–13 cm (4–5 inches) cold water and stir to remove residual heat which, when cooking in larger quantities, can sometimes curdle the sauce.

6 Allow the custard to cool completely, sprinkling the surface with a little caster sugar to prevent a skin forming.

7 When cold, whisk in the sugar on the top, then fold in the cream. Ⓐ

8 Ladle over the trifle biscuits. Cover with cling film and chill until ready to decorate.

9 To make the topping, whip the cream with the brandy and sugar until it stands in soft peaks. Do not overwhip or it will become too wet for piping. Fill half the cream into a large piping bag fitted with a rose tube. Spread the remaining cream ad lib over the trifle surface, then pipe a neat collar round the rim of each trifle.

10 Spike alternate rows of ratafias and almonds into the cream. Arrange the glacé fruits and angelica pieces ad lib. Chill until ready to serve. Ⓐ

11 Stand each trifle on an under plate, lined with a folded linen napkin or paper doily.

Ⓐ The trifle sponges can be prepared 2–3 days in advance and stored in an airtight container. The custard can be made 1 day ahead, covered and kept chilled. The trifle should not be completed more than 4 hours before serving.

RICH VELVET CHOCOLATE CREAMS

SERVES 20

300 g (14 oz) plain chocolate
2 whole eggs (size 1)
2 egg yolks (size 1)
350 ml (12 fl oz) single cream
350 ml (12 fl oz) double cream
120 ml (4 fl oz) Crème de Cacao or Drambuie
50 ml (2 fl oz) brandy or whisky

DECORATION:
chocolate beans, buttons or crumbled flaked chocolate bar

PREPARATION TIME: 1 hour, 20 minutes, plus chilling overnight

Ideally this rich velvety mousse should be made in small chocolate pots, sherry glasses, coffee cups or simple plain plastic cartons.

When you want to be extra-indulgent, top with whipped cream or serve double cream separately.

1 Melt the chocolate in a large 7 litre (12 pint) heatproof bowl over simmering water.

2 In a second heatproof bowl whisk the eggs and yolks together, then arrange this over a second pan of simmering water (or the same pan after you've melted the chocolate). Using a balloon whisk, whisk the eggs until the texture of a good custard. Stand the basin in a sink containing 10–12 cm (4–5 inches) of cold water. Whisk for a minute or so to remove the residual heat.

3 Cool both mixtures, whisking from time to time to prevent setting. When both are cooled to the same temperature, whisk the egg mixture into the large bowl of melted chocolate.

4 In another bowl whisk the 2 creams and liqueurs to soft-peak. A

5 Cut and fold the cream mixture thoroughly into the chocolate. Ladle into 20 individual containers (or 2 large ones). Place the containers on a tray, cover with cling film and chill overnight.

18th Century ratafia trifle; Rich velvet chocolate creams

6 On the day of serving, uncover and decorate at will.

A The cream can be whipped the day before, covered with cling film and kept chilled.

Index